How Love Works

A new approach to lasting partnership

Jeff & Sue Allen

with Helena Foss

Balloonview

Printed and bound in Great Britain by
CPI Group (UK) Ltd, Croydon, CR0 4YY

ISBN 978-1-907798-24-5

Sue and Jeff hold regular online workshops and are committed to your happy relationship. For further details of events, help with relationships or questions about any of the principles in this book visit www.visionworksforlife.com or email info@visionworksforlife.com

About The Authors

Sue & Jeff Allen run Psychology of Vision seminars, trainings, counselling and business consultancy in the UK, Europe and the Far East. Sue's background is in educational publishing and Jeff was once a cargo sailor. They live in Wiltshire and have two grown up children. They have been married for 33 years.

Contents

'It's the heart afraid of breaking that never learns to dance.'
Bette Midler

'The salvation of man is through love and in love.'
Viktor Frankl

Acknowledgements

Much of the wisdom in this book comes from seminars and books written by Lency Spezzano, MS, and Chuck Spezzano, Ph D., and from teachings in A Course in Miracles. Our thanks to Lency and Chuck, for your guidance and infinite patience with us as slow learners.

Thanks also to Helena Foss. Your confidence in us was the catalyst for this project; you kick-started us to express ourselves and merged your voice with ours.

And to all our family, friends, fellow trainers, workshop participants and clients – every single one of you has contributed something to the tapestry of this book. Some of you know the details close up, some of you have a more distant view; we know there is more in store.

Above all, unlimited love and gratitude to our children for choosing us, and witnessing us wrestle with life and with each other.

Thanks also to our friend Pam Carruthers for the Shrek 3 story in Chapter 2.

Note From The Co-Author

I first met Jeff and Sue Allen when hitting problems in my own relationship. As a freelance feature writer, my personal turmoil had inspired to me to research relationship therapies and the effects they were having. I looked at everything from traditional couples counselling to more outlandish methods such as shamanism and tantra. Of all the couples I interviewed, Sue and Jeff's story was by far the most compelling.

I believe that the Psychology of Vision (PoV) model which Jeff and Sue teach has an important contribution to make to the world of relationship counselling. Because of its 'spiritual' components, such as the principles of forgiveness and the concept of oneness (the idea that we are all indelibly connected and therefore reflections of each other) it has yet to catch on in mainstream consciousness. In my opinion, it is time for that to change.

The people I have met in the PoV workshops I have participated in are anything but kooky new agers. Most are well educated and successful in their chosen field. But that is not enough for them. They seem driven by a deeper desire to work out exactly what is going on in our relationships and how we can apply that to the problems the world faces today. Because, let's face it, there has to be a better way forward. Whether it be in our most intimate relationships or on the world political stage, it is time to learn to stop the fighting. As Gandhi said, 'Be the change you want to see in the world'. If global conflict distresses you, as it does me, then the best place – indeed the only place – to start, is with yourself and those closest to your heart.

In my former career as a hypnotherapist, I became intimately acquainted with the workings of the subconscious mind. The PoV model, however, has taken my understanding of it to another level entirely. It is the most comprehensive, intricate and insightful model of human relating I have come across. This book outlines the main principles of what could surely be a new model for relating in the 21st Century. Not quite a revolution, it is more of an evolution in our collective consciousness. It is my hope that this book moves that evolution on so that it can be embraced by established psychotherapy trainings and, indeed, our whole education system. This is the kind of education I wish for my young son. May he, and all our children, enjoy healthy, happy, loving relationships and co-create a better way of living together than we, as a species, have managed so far.

Helena Foss
www.helenafoss.co.uk

Part One:

THERE HAS TO BE A BETTER WAY

'The unexamined life is not worth living.'
Socrates

Chapter 1:

INTRODUCTION

Our Story

Sue says:

It is now over 20 years since I served divorce papers on Jeff back in 1990, ten years into our marriage. At the time I was in a state of utter despair. I had spent every ounce of energy I had putting on a brave face for my family, my friends and the world in general. I kept pretending everything was OK until I was just too exhausted to live the lie any longer. Admitting defeat was devastating, but it was also such a relief to finally throw in the towel.

I wanted to draw a line under the whole sorry mess, put all those painful feelings behind me and move on. What I didn't realise then, however, was that I wasn't actually 'moving on' at all. All those painful feelings still needed looking at and resolving. I would have just taken them all into my next relationship.

Jeff was my second husband so this was the second time I had lost my 'true love' and both splits had involved other women. What was going on? Why did I always attract men who betrayed me?

This book is about both my and Jeff's journey to finding the answers to our marriage problems.

My personal journey has hardly been a walk in the park; at times it has been hellish. But for all the agony, I would not change a thing. I am eternally grateful I took the risk to let Jeff back into my life. In terms of personal happiness, the rewards have been beyond anything I ever dreamed of.

Jeff says:

As a young, macho sailor with, quite literally at one time, a woman in every port, I used to see myself as a wild and independent free spirit. I had a 'man's gotta do what a man's gotta do' attitude to my marriage and my young family. It was only when it was all about to be taken away from me that I finally broke out of my denial. I had thought that I didn't need anyone or anything. But then life gave me a stark choice: carry on with my so-called independent, fancy-free life, or commit to my wife and two children.

The agony of making this decision kept me awake for many nights, thoughts whirling round my mind, as I tried to make sense of it all. I believed I was invincible: climb any mountain, sail any sea, fight any beast. But when it came to my emotions, I was a quivering wreck. It took all my courage to commit to working things out with Sue, but the results have been priceless. As well as being in a happy, committed relationship, this difficult journey has also led to an extraordinarily rewarding career. This is our story and it is a bit of a rollercoaster. We welcome you on board. Please, sit back and enjoy the ride!

Our Roots as Relationship Experts

We met in 1974 and married in 1979 when Sue was pregnant with our first child. In 1990 we separated for two years. It was our personal journeys with Psychology of Vision that brought us back from the brink of divorce. We now teach what we have learned and, to date, have worked with a combined total of about 750 private clients and roughly 10,000 workshop participants both in the UK and abroad. It seems timely to put all our theory, experience and knowledge into book form.

Some people call us relationship experts. One definition of an expert is a person who has made every single mistake in a narrow field. If that is the case, then yes, we can claim the 'expert' mantle. We have learned the hard way what it takes to make a marriage work in the long term.

We know now that learning to have good relationships is the foundation for a happy and successful life. Happy relationships are the wings beneath our feet, whereas the weight of unhappy relationships sinks us. We also know that it is not a matter of luck: there are skills and principles that we can use every day to make good relationships possible. It is this knowledge and skills base we want to pass on to you.

Sue says:

After Jeff and I split up I gave up on the dream of a happy relationship. I had some success in business; I was self-employed and working from home, with an educational publishing company and simultaneously a booming nursery school we set up in an outbuilding partly to 'child-mind' our two children. But the field of relationships was a disaster. I seemed destined to bounce around between lovers, in a haphazard quest to find some peace and happiness. It felt impossible to understand what someone else thought or wanted, or anticipate the next random threat to lasting commitment. I felt I had disappointed my parents who had celebrated my two weddings and supported me as best they could, and I had certainly disappointed myself. Most of all I had been disappointed by my husbands: both were not the partners I wanted them to be, both seemed irresponsibly unfaithful to our vows and impossible to communicate with in any meaningful way without someone getting angry or distant (them) or emotional and heartbroken (me).

The more I complained about my situation to my friends, or to anyone who would listen, the worse I felt. More than one potential suitor was totally put off by my suffering which only seemed to solidify my heartbreak and reinforce my picture of myself as a well-intentioned, wronged and powerless victim. Increasingly, I invested my emotional life in our two young children; it seemed safe and easy to love them unreservedly.

I remember clearly the moment of hope in my heart when all this changed. I was, as usual, talking about my situation with my sister whose support was complete and irreplaceable.

Suddenly I came to the word 'failed' and I realised how difficult it was for me to even utter the word. To admit that I had f.. f... failed in my relationships was almost impossible to accept. I had spent so much time and energy blaming my partners and building myself up as the 'good' one. Accepting my failure felt like an emotional earthquake, a violent tectonic shift. The same moment I realised my own part in our broken family, I simultaneously let go of the dream of Jeff being the kind of partner and father to our children that I wanted him to be. Suddenly I felt so light and free: free to be myself, free to let Jeff be himself, free to move into a different future.

Could the lifeline to change be so simple?

The answer is 'yes', the lifeline to things starting to change was that simple but profound shift in attitude. Soon after this, on a Monday morning after attending a 3 day Psychology of Vision weekend workshop, Jeff visited us at home and he was different. Suddenly everything wasn't all my fault, I wasn't the biggest mistake of his life and he was talking about his part in the hell we had created. He seemed softer to me, more willing to listen than rant.

Of course it took me a few more months to admit to him that I would trust this change. Let's be honest, I held out partly in revenge for all the waiting I had done in the past, and also because I wanted Jeff to prove the new attitude would stick before I agreed to give our relationship another chance.

We know now that as soon as one partner gives up being right and holding onto their position, then the other partner does the same to the same degree. We also get the dynamics of our particular situation, of how our marriage had failed. And we know that understanding how relationships work and applying the principles in our daily lives is the key to success.

The lifeline for us was the idea that it is possible to learn this skill, and we want this book to be your lifeline. We hope some phrase, principle, story or exercise gives you that moment of hope in your heart that can be your springboard to greater happiness.

Since we recommitted to our marriage we have continued to learn many lessons of course. We have learned from our work with clients, from our workshops and writings, from our children and from our own relationship which is still evolving. All of that information we have put in this book, distilled as simply as possible and intended to be useful in your life.

Our Teachers

The bedrock of our success, both in our relationship and our work, is the wisdom of our friends and teachers, the American therapists Chuck and Lency Spezzano, who together developed Psychology of Vision (PoV). PoV is a depth psychology model that is taught and practised internationally. It has helped thousands of people find meaning in their lives and given them the tools to change. PoV is based on the principles of love and forgiveness, as set out in A Course in Miracles (ACIM), a practical manual of spiritual psychology written by Helen Schucman and William Thetford, who have since both died. At the time, they were Professors of Medical Psychology at Columbia University's

College of Physicians and Surgeons in New York City. First published in 1976, the manual has since become an international phenomenon.

ACIM has had a profound influence not just on us and the international PoV community, but on the world. In his inaugural speech, Nelson Mandela famously quoted a paragraph from 'A Return to Love: Reflections on the Principles of A Course in Miracles' by Marianne Williamson, the prominent American ACIM teacher and best-selling author. You may remember it from one of those inspirational 'pass-it-on' emails that people forward to their friends:

'Our deepest fear is not that we are inadequate. Our deepest fear is that we are powerful beyond measure. It is our light, not our darkness that most frightens us. We ask ourselves: Who am I to be brilliant, gorgeous, talented, fabulous? Actually, who are you not to be? You are a child of God. Your playing small does not serve the world. There is nothing enlightened about shrinking so that other people won't feel insecure around you. We are all meant to shine, as children do. We were born to make manifest the glory of God that is within us. It's not just in some of us; it's in everyone. And as we let our own light shine, we unconsciously give other people permission to do the same. As we are liberated from our own fear, our presence automatically liberates others.'

In our workshops, both in the UK and abroad, we have seen this principle at work many times. Deep down, most of us are programmed to believe we are somehow flawed, bad or downright worthless. We get so used to this subtle yet bottom-line inner programming that it becomes our norm, our modus operandi.

Through his work with thousands of clients, PoV co-founder, Chuck Spezzano learned that the deepest fear people have is the fear of 'having it all' and of being all we can be. We get stuck, addicted even, to having a life full of problems and barriers that hold us back. It is somehow easier to stay small. In fact, we can all have whatever we want – but only when 100 per cent of us wants it. We can bust through limiting self-judgments – and, like Mandela, we can even triumph over oppression, if we dare keep our integrity and our hearts set on the goals we know are absolutely true for us.

The Origins of Psychology of Vision

It was Chuck Spezzano's nuts and bolts approach to relationship counselling that held our attention from the first workshops we attended, first separately and then together. Chuck is a visionary, articulate and hilarious teacher who inspires us because it is so obvious he has experienced what he teaches. He also has this way of connecting with you which makes you feel loved and supported, even while you are admitting your innermost fears or inadequacies.

At the age of 20, Chuck was training to be a Catholic priest in a seminary in Pittsburgh, Philadelphia. He says: *'I was always looking for answers as to why my family was so dysfunctional. As a child I could sense the pain my parents and siblings were in, yet felt at a loss as to how to help them, so I vowed that as an adult, I would do everything I could to help people get out of pain. When I realised the priesthood couldn't teach me this, I left the seminary and did three things: Firstly, I started training as a counselling psychologist. Secondly, I went out and did the 'fieldwork' by having relationships and making lots of mistakes. Lastly, I prayed for a book that would teach me how to have wonderful, loving relationships and bring me home to my spiritual heart at the same time.'*

'I began developing Psychology of Vision whilst working at a rehabilitation centre for war veterans and marines with drug and authority issues. When our therapy budgets got cut, I started developing my intuitive method of accessing the deeper subconscious mind, so that I could make much quicker and more effective psychological interventions. I was amazed and even shocked at some of the answers that came up from the deeper mind.'

Finally, after eight years as a therapist, a colleague suggested Chuck read A Course in Miracles. *'It was such a joy for me to discover the book I had been praying for,'* he adds. *'There were principles in there which could not be found anywhere else in psychological literature, and which corroborated and affirmed what I was already doing intuitively. It provided the spiritual element that I could see was so sorely needed for therapy to be truly effective. I am still learning from ACIM and expect that I will continue to do so for the rest of my life.'*

Later we met Chuck's empathic wife Lency. Her feminine approach brings another dimension to the Psychology of Vision model, which they have built together over the last 30 years, and which forms the basis of much of the material in this book. Their work is fuelled by and intertwined with their relationship and is a living, evolving example of how love works.

The term Psychology of Vision means being able to see beyond our own personal suffering and see the bigger picture, from a higher spiritual viewpoint. Being able to do this, we believe, is one of the reasons Nelson Mandela has become something of a living saint. Mandela's great contribution to humanity was refusing to take revenge on the people who had persecuted him and his fellow South Africans so mercilessly, because he could see that this was what the 'bigger picture' – the future wellbeing of his country – required. Despite his own personal anguish, he knew that the only way forward was truth, reconciliation and, ultimately, forgiveness.

The same 'big picture' potential applies to every relationship. If we are stuck in relationship hell, feeling that our partner is our biggest block to happiness and wanting revenge, we poison ourselves and our environment with bitterness. The American writer Malachy McCourt said, *'Resentment is like drinking poison and waiting for the other person to die.'* The toxicity spreads to our children and families, the energy of it multiplies. If we can move towards seeing our partner as on the same team as us, as a fellow traveler with whom it is possible to find a better way, then the potential for the relationship is limitless and it ripples out to nourish our children and families instead.

How to Use This Book

Although this book is aimed primarily at people who are hitting problems in their relationship, it is also for everyone who wants to know what it takes to have a great relationship. Whether you have one currently or not, are madly in love or at each other's throats, and especially if you are feeling heartbroken by a former partner, you will gain many insights from the information we present here.

How Love Works is partly a memoir - we relate our own experiences as a couple - and also a compilation of stories. The examples we give from clients and workshop participants to illustrate the principles, are composites and we have changed the names. At times we suggest exercises or questions, because we want the principles to be practical in your daily life, not just nice ideas.

We outline the common mistakes and assumptions we all make in relationships, debunking the many myths about true love that are endemic in our culture. We then take you through the anatomy of a typical relationship; navigating the mazes, stages, perils, traps, pitfalls and joys that await us all on the road to true intimacy. The same principles apply to all relationships, whether heterosexual or homosexual – and also to our relationships with friends, siblings, parents, carers, step-family and children.

If you are struggling with your relationship right now, maybe feeling despondent or depressed about your future together, then just understanding the dynamics that are being played out between you and your partner can be really helpful. Take it from us, it is such a relief to 'get' why things seem to have got so bad with the person you were once convinced was the one for you.

In Part Four, the final section of the book, we outline what we believe to be the new paradigm of relating for the 21st century. We have rewritten the unspoken 'rules' of relating because, quite frankly, the old way just doesn't work anymore. It is, as the saying goes, completely unsustainable. It is time for humanity to move on, from blaming, shaming and fighting, to finding resolution, harmony and love in the unlikeliest of places; the private and individual power struggle of a committed partnership.

All we ask is that you, the reader, keep an open mind, right to the very end of this book. Many of the principles that we work with, and refer to, require a shift in some of our most basic core beliefs about life and how it works. It has taken us many years to integrate these principles into our lives and so we don't expect you to assimilate them all straightaway.

However, it is our hope that this book becomes your reference tool, your guide and friend that you can turn to in the darkest depths of hopelessness and despair, when the light seems to have truly disappeared from your relationship – and a manual for how to do it better. There has to be a better way – and this is our version of what that better way is. It works for us. Our deepest wish is that it helps you find sustainable, lasting happiness too.

Chapter 2:

WHAT IS GOING WRONG WITH RELATIONSHIPS?

Good relationships are the bedrock upon which our society is based - and upon which we build our lives. Good relationships breed successful teams at work and successful families at home; they correlate to good physical and mental health and feelings of fulfillment and happiness. There has been much bemoaning in recent years of the fact that as divorce rates rise, the family unit is falling apart and therefore breaking up the fabric of society. Politicians have offered tax incentives to encourage married couples to stay together. But it takes far, far more than a cash bonus to make a marriage work.

According to the UK Office of National Statistics, divorce rates in 2005 suggested that approximately 45 per cent of all marriages will end in divorce. Of these, almost half will occur before the couple's tenth anniversary.

Of the marriages that do stay intact, many are held together by psychological sticky tape. Many of us have become adept at papering over the cracks (sometimes yawning chasms) of differences and conflict. People settle for a 'better than nothing' marriage, rather than be alone. There may well be couples who have reached their Ruby wedding anniversary 'without a cross word between them' but we, personally, haven't met any. We suspect that many of them have compromised to the point that they simply don't speak at all. Loving couples are the exception and not the rule.

It is rare to find a truly committed, loving couple whose bond strengthens over the years. These people will most likely tell you it has involved a lot of highs, lows and sheer hard work to reach that level of intimacy and keep their love alive. For most of us, relationships are a struggle. They can, in fact, be one of the most difficult challenges of our lives.

This is because, in your relationship, your partner is functioning as a mirror to your deeper self. It is our experience that the best way to learn about yourself, the best and fastest way to grow and develop as a person - and also to grow spiritually - is through relationships.

Whilst your relationship with yourself is incredibly important (without a respectable level of self-love you will not do well in any relationship), we still need others to reflect who we are back to us. Otherwise we literally cannot see the wood for the trees – our behaviour is often so automatic that we cannot see it until someone else points it out. And whilst we might love being our independent, individual, kooky selves, we really are nothing without our friends and family.

Jeff says:

In 2002 we were in Nairobi and we visited an elephant orphanage close to the city. There were about a dozen baby or young elephants and their keepers explained that unless a keeper slept alongside each elephant every night the elephant would die. Without nurturing and bonding even a well-fed and sheltered elephant will not survive. We humans are the same; without human nurturing and affection we also die, probably biologically and certainly emotionally and spiritually.

> We have also found this supported in our work. Many people have developed the construct that they were brought up in these terrible circumstances with all these terrible things happening to them. While it might be true that many regrettable things happened, it was not the norm and the evidence of this is that we must have had moments of nurturing and affection, which resulted in times of happiness and joy, because we are still alive. In my times of independence, I was convinced that I needed no-one, even to the point of sailing for quite long times alone and this worked great until I had no-one and then the deep painful feelings of old hurt came up. We all have painful feelings buried in our minds, but what makes us safe are our friends, our family, our partners and the human contact that we secretly crave every day.

The Dalai Lama has been quoted as saying that we only truly exist through our relationships with others. '*We can live without religion and meditation,*' says this master of meditation and head of the Tibetan Buddhist religion, '*but we cannot survive without human affection.*' One reason for this, we propose, is because, ultimately, we are not separate beings. On a deeper level, as ACIM says, we are all indelibly connected and, therefore, here to grow and learn from each other. (And yes, that also includes that ratbag who cheated on you, or the evil cow who humiliated you in front of your friends.) It is actually unnatural to live a completely isolated life – and life can be brutal. All our lives will contain some level of pain and heartbreak. Why? In order for you to grow, by practising compassion towards both yourself and others. The Dalai Lama describes this as the religion of kindness.

In our work we have seen time and again that every single relationship – even if it ends in heartbreak – has a purpose. It is trying to teach you something about yourself; something that you can only see when it is reflected back to you through the mirror of your partner. It is easy to blame an ex or current partner for making you miserable, but if there is a pattern to your relationships, if the same kind of issues keep coming up in your relationships over and over again, then it's time to wake up to what is going on; because the common denominator is *you*. If you are willing to look honestly at what it is inside you, that is keeping you stuck in this particular pattern, then this book can help you work out what drives that pattern and how to break free of it.

Client Story:

There was always someone in Marie's life whose lateness drove her crazy. It was stressful because she felt she had to be on time for this person, also knowing she would have to wait for them. When they showed up she tried not to be angry but she was upset by their rudeness and lack of consideration for her, and she realised this issue had soured every relationship.

We helped Marie to intuitively remember back to the first time she had felt the stress of punctuality. How old had she been? Who else had been there with her when this situation first happened? Marie remembered how, when she was three years old, she and her mother had made an emergency dash to her grandfather's bedside, only to miss the moment of his death by minutes. The emotional memory of her mother's distress and her own grief of being unable to help, had stayed within her all these years, this past pain literally torturing her in the present. As a three year old, Marie had decided that being late was agonizingly stressful, and she had made the choice that from then on she would never ever be late.

Once Marie realised the connection between this story and a major pattern of her relationships, she was able to release the emotional pain of the past. She also made the choice to reclaim her power rather than feel at the mercy of time and another person's lateness.

✓ Try this:

Think for a moment about your relationships. Is there a pattern you can identify, one that resurfaces again and again even though each partner or friend seems so different? Recognising and naming a pattern gives us two vital keys: one, when we stop to ask ourselves when was the very first time we felt this way, we see that the pattern started for us long before we ever met this person and, two, we can change any pattern if we are willing to take responsibility, find the root of it, and apply a healing principle which helps us break free.

Of course, not all marriages or relationships are meant to last for life. But this doesn't mean you need to get locked into the kind of bitter divorce battle that the tabloids love to splash all over their front pages (and which many of us secretly enjoy reading as it makes our own relationship failures seem more bearable). Instead, you can learn how to become friends and separate amicably. This is an essential skill, especially if you share a social circle and, most importantly, if there are children involved. Whatever the outcome, we will show you that love can always prevail.

The Myths About Love

The path of love is no easy ride. Relationships are tough and many couples don't make it. So what is going on? Why is true love so hard to find and why do we have to suffer so many devastating heartbreaks along the way? The kind of heartbreaks that feel like our world is collapsing around us, like the ground is trembling beneath our feet. We grow up with so many misconstrued ideas about what love is and how relationships work, it is actually quite shocking to realise how deluded we are. Here are, in no particular order, our 'top six' popular myths about love relationships.

Myth No 1: Relationships 'just happen'

What were you taught in school about how to have a happy, loving relationship? We are simply not educated about it. For something that is supposed to form the bedrock and fabric of society, it is astonishing how glaringly absent it is from the national curriculum. Instead, there is an assumption that, just like new parenthood, we will somehow just know what to do when it arrives in our lives. It will all just come naturally. When it does happen, we are then hit with the realisation that we actually haven't got a clue. We hit the ground running, learn on the job, make lots of mistakes and muddle through as best we can.

The way we currently learn about relationships is through the role models in our lives; namely, our parents. With the best will in the world, many of them were not well equipped with the essential skills – let alone educated in the *art* – of healthy relating. There is a belief that our happiness depends on finding the right partner. This is true to an extent, but it is more accurate to say that our happiness depends on how we relate to our partner once we have committed to them.

How often do we read of impulsive marriages that last a very short time, in at least one celebrity case just twenty-four hours? We can identify with the couple's spontaneous exuberance, and also with their crushing disappointment once the honeymoon feeling ends and they experience it as a horrible mistake.

In dating or marriage, if you think the first argument means the relationship is over then your relationships are bound to be very short, and probably getting shorter all the time. Time to realise that when the honeymoon feeling ends the relationship isn't over – on the contrary, it is time to go to work !

Myth No 2: Your prince or princess will come and you will both live happily ever after

This is the ending to numerous childhood fairy tales that many of us grew up hearing last thing at night, just before we dropped off to sleep. At this point, any good hypnotherapist can practically hear the phrase drop like a stone into the impressionable child's subconscious mind, to live on into adulthood as an accepted truth. The implication is that once you find the love of your life, then that is it; you will be happy, fulfilled and complete forevermore. Let's be honest here: how often have you really seen that happen, in your own life or in the lives of others close to you? Anyone in a relationship like that is very lucky indeed.

'Rom com' movies are some of the worst offenders in perpetuating this myth. These movies typically end with the couple finally kissing passionately and declaring their undying love for each other. Metaphorically speaking, the screen couple waves a merry goodbye to the camera and skips off, hand in hand, into the sunset. It might be the ending in the movie, but in the real, gritty world of relating, falling in love and getting married are just the beginning. It's when the honeymoon is over that some of us think, to our horror: 'Oh no, this is not how I imagined it would be,' worrying that we have made the most dreadful mistake. Again, getting together is the easy bit; it is once the honeymoon is over that the work really starts.

Myth No 3: Your partner exists to save you from your pain

There is a scene in the movie 'Shrek 3' when, trapped in a prison, the fairy tale princesses hatch a cunning plan to escape:

Snow White: *'Right! Ladies, assume the position!'* (Sleeping Beauty falls asleep, Rapunzel sits on a high stool with her braid trailing, Snow White lies down in her coffin pose, and Cinderella seats herself on the floor gazing dreamily into space.)

Princess Fiona: *'What are you doing?'*

Snow White: (exasperated) *'Waiting to be rescued!'*

Isn't that what we have all, at some level, been taught about love? For women especially, the idea of being saved and whisked away by a hunky knight remains rather alluring. That and the idea that your wedding day is the most special day of your life (presumably it is all downhill from there)! One of the biggest mistakes we make in relationships is assuming that our partner exists on this earth to meet all our needs and save us from our pain, loneliness and despair. That is one heck of a responsibility and not one that anyone can realistically live up to. Mr or Ms Right is not actually your missing piece – but they can turn out to be the key that unlocks your inner world, enabling you, ultimately, to save yourself.

Myth No 4: True love will make you happy

This myth is so prevalent, it might as well be etched in stone. We cannot seem to let go of the notion that true love will save us. Wistfully we think: 'If only I had true love, then my life would be happy, perfect and complete.' The real purpose of relationship is to understand and then heal the wounded parts of ourselves. Only when we are able to do that, will we be happy.

As we said before, your partner is your mirror to your unhealed self. No-one will be able to push your buttons as easily as he or she can. Everything that is broken in our minds will, at some point or other, show up within our relationship for us to look at and heal.

Myth No 5: When things get difficult, the relationship is over

When things get difficult, the relationship is starting! It is after the honeymoon that the real work begins.

In our workshops we have met many people who say they want a relationship but when they look a little deeper, they realise that the thought of falling in love, and once more opening up and being vulnerable is, quite frankly, terrifying. They are just too scared to go there again. A part of them wants a relationship, but another part has put the brakes on. (This happens at a subconscious level and we will explain how this works later.) They end up being attracted to potential partners who are unavailable; they might be married, living abroad or unable to commit. The result is that they end up checking into heartbreak hotel yet again and sinking into a pit of despair. Why oh why, they wonder, do my relationships never work out?

Client Story:

When we met Jane, she said she had spent years searching for Mr Perfect. It took some time to convince her that no such person existed and that her search for the impossible perfect partner actually masked her fear of finding *any* partner. When we took a deeper look, Jane's underlying fear of her own imperfection was revealed. On the surface she was looking for someone who would make her happy but underneath it all she felt herself to be flawed and incapable of true happiness.

Real, long term love is not for the faint-hearted. It requires you to open your heart right up and when you do so, any old sadness and pain that has been laying unexpressed, will inflict itself upon you to be felt and released. You cannot open up your heart without, at some point, going through all the reasons it closed down in the first place.

Awakening to your heart means awakening to your suffering too. Heartbreaks break your heart open. No matter how hard your relationship – or your heartbreak – feels, there is a lesson there that will, at some point down the line, make perfect sense, if you can look at it from the right perspective.

Myth No 6: If only my partner would change, then I would be happy

Oh dear. The classic heffalump trap we all fall into when the honeymoon stage is over and the niggles and fights begin. It was Dr Wayne Dyer who coined the phrase: '*When you change the way you look at things, the things you look at change.*' This applies to relationships too. Do you like being nagged and lectured to about your faults? Does nagging and criticising someone inspire them to change or does it inspire them to do the very opposite: stick to their guns and defend themselves?

Forcing someone to change in order to make you happy is not love, it is need and in the long run it never works. If you want your partner to change, the best place to start is with yourself. The payoff is that when you change, magically, they do too. They *have* to change to keep relating to the 'new' you. (Don't worry if all this sounds confusing, we will explain it all later on in the book.)

As we have said before, true love will *not* save you from your pain. Quite the opposite; it will *bring up* all your unresolved pain. The responsibility for this pain is yours alone – not your partner's, no matter how much they look like they are to blame. Even if your partner did (begrudgingly) change for you, your pain would still be there and would, no doubt, hook itself onto someone else or get played out in some other situation.

If you still don't believe us, then keep on nagging your partner and demanding that they change. Then see how far it gets you. Good luck! (You'll need it.)

Unless you have lived without watching any movies, sitcoms, soap operas, listening to pop music, or reading any fairy tales or romantic novels, you probably have consciously or subconsciously bought into one or all of these Myths.

We humans are story-telling creatures. We can see the power of our collective myths when a royal wedding takes place in the UK. Millions watched Prince Charles' wedding to Diana and, more recently, the marriage of Prince William and Kate Middleton. This is not necessarily because the British Royal family is so fascinating; but because such occasions also speak to the mythical part of each one of us. Who of us has not dreamed of finding our prince or princess? Even if we have lost touch with these beliefs, the pageantry still affects us in a way we don't always understand but can certainly learn about.

✓ Try this:

Think of your present relationship, and if you don't have one right now then think of your last relationship. Bring to mind your last argument or time that you felt bad about something. Was one of these myths at play? Did you have a picture of how love should be that your partner wasn't living up to?

Look at the situation again through new eyes and ask yourself, which dream of romance or myth of love were you expecting?

Now ask yourself, when did this myth start for you? Probably the answer is long before you met your partner.

Are you willing now to let go of this picture rather than impose it on your relationship?

You know when you have let go because you feel different, lighter and more open for some other solution.

The New Paradigm of Relationships

Marriage vows have got it all wrong. The first one should read: '*Is this the person you are willing to go to hell and back with a thousand times to heal all the fractures in your mind?*'

It's time to dispel the myths about love and get real about what it is really like at the coalface of relationships. It is hard, it can be arduous, but it is absolutely worth it. But first we need to understand what is going on: Why do our relationships get into such a mess? Why are there so many divorces and so many unhappy marriages? Why so much heartbreak?

Before we even get to the stages and dynamics of relationships in Part Two of this book, we need to understand the invisible forces that drive all relationships and, indeed, all human behaviour. We need to understand the forces of the subconscious mind.

Chapter 3

THE INVISIBLE FORCES THAT DRIVE ALL RELATIONSHIPS

In his book 'The Feeling of What Happens', Antonio Damasio, Professor of neurology at the University of Iowa College of Medicine, suggests that we are all driven primarily by our emotions. It is our emotions, according to Damasio, that mould our consciousness, our very sense of who we are.

We all behave because of how we feel underneath. If you have already decided that we have something worthwhile to say, then you will probably read this book right through to the end. But if you felt that it doesn't agree with your ideas, would you read it? We doubt it. It's more likely that once you get to an idea that you find challenging or uncomfortable, you would lose interest or get impatient and eventually stop reading it.

Relationships are highly emotive experiences. You can have a high IQ and a wealth of academic qualifications under your belt, but that is no guarantee of success in your love life, nor, indeed, in life in general.

In his landmark book 'Emotional Intelligence' Daniel Goleman cites research that suggests that only 20 per cent of our worldly success can be attributed to our IQ. The rest directly correlates to our levels of emotional maturity.

Client Story:

George was desperate when he approached us. As a successful businessman, he valued his ability to solve problems. Not only did he expect himself to have a high level of intelligence and achievement, but also he expected it of others. He had built a strong, winning team around him. They set their goals and drove themselves to achieve them without thought of anything else. In George's mind he had created the ultimate team of like minded people and he was not in a position to listen to any negative or questioning feedback and certainly had no place for discussing feelings or other wet and unproductive subjects.

Then to the great surprise of the whole team one of their members committed suicide. It was a shock to everyone but business continued as usual. Certainly they paid their respects to the family and recruited a replacement but no one spoke of the incident and basically everyone distanced himself or herself from it. All went well for a while but slowly the team became increasingly ineffective, the buzz had gone and each task seemed to take massive amounts of energy. They started to lose contracts. George with his analytical mind was confounded; he knew something was wrong but had no idea how to address it. All his efforts to transform this problem came to nought. And now he was beginning to feel depressed and thoughts of failure started to creep into his mind.

George, with zero emotional intelligence, needed to learn some lessons quickly. Firstly, one of the reasons people commit suicide is because they feel really bad or feel like a failure and are mostly depressed, almost the same feelings as George was now beginning to experience. Not only did he feel bad, but everyone in the team felt the same way and if they had had the chance to share their deepest thoughts and feelings everyone would have spoken of their guilt, their bad feelings, for not being there to support their colleague, of not being aware of how someone they were working so closely with actually felt. This team guilt had not been addressed. Guilt makes people withdraw, and as they pull back every job becomes difficult and ineffective. Basically everyone had built a wall to try and protect themselves from this sea of unresolved emotions.

George finally started to recognise the importance of emotional intelligence and the need to increase his awareness of how people were feeling around him. He also learned that there was no reason to blame himself for his colleague's actions. These were very important lessons which, once he acted on them and brought them into his team, gave meaning and relevance to his colleague's death.

Our emotions drive our behaviour, despite our best attempts at rationalizing and explaining things 'logically'. Not one of us acts randomly. We all behave in a manner that reflects how we feel underneath. When we feel good, it is easy to behave well; when we feel bad, we tend to impose those bad feelings on the people around us in some way or another. When we become aware of how we are feeling and recognise why we do what we do, we can also see why others do what they do. It is our EQ (emotional intelligence) rather than our IQ that counts when it comes to being successful in both love and life.

Every one of us has had times in our relationships when we have lashed out in a moment of anger. We may be mortified by such an emotional eruption and work hard to repress similar future outbursts. But repressing our emotions is a poor strategy.

Sue says:

> Suppressed anger was certainly a feature of our relationship before we broke up. It seemed every time we tried to break through the brick wall of cold silence and really talk about stuff it would spiral into a huge argument. The intensity of the emotion scared us. As we glimpsed the smorgasbord of unresolved emotion on display, principally guilt, we started on the blame game and we would drag all our past mistakes into the fray. So it felt like going round in circles and eventually we just gave up.

In her book 'Why Good People Do Bad Things', the American writer Debbie Ford likens emotional repression to what she calls the Beach-Ball Effect. You can only hold an inflatable ball down in the water for so long before it bounces back up and either splashes or hits you or someone else in the face. Emotions have an energy to them that has to be managed or channeled appropriately. If, on the other hand, you choose to deaden yourself to your volatile emotions, then you create distance between you and your partner and the relationship becomes stuck. Either way, no-one moves forward towards happiness and success.

Our positive emotions lead to positive outcomes and these don't require any change. We don't spend hours talking to our friends or therapists about what goes right. So what is this inner world of painful feelings that we keep talking about? What forces keep our emotional triggers in place? It is called the subconscious mind and it wields an extraordinary power over our lives that most of us are barely aware of.

The Power of Your Subconscious Mind

We all like to think that we are in the driving seat of our lives, in control of everything we say or do, but in reality what we see in others' and our own behaviours is merely the tip of the iceberg.

Only this small percentage of our minds is actually conscious and making rational decisions. Everything else is part of the vast subconscious mind that lurks underneath the surface of our conscious awareness. This is known as the mental iceberg, which postulates that there is a lot more going on within us than shows above the surface. This hidden aspect of us, if not realised, can do great damage to our 'ship', just as the unseen portions of the icebergs of our beliefs and the 'baggage' we bring into a relationship, can do great damage if we do not recognise them.

In the model below, the top level represents everything that happens to us, what other people do with us, to us or at us, it includes our conscious world.

But our conscious behaviour is driven by our emotions and feelings. We act and behave because of how we feel and so does everyone else around us. If we don't look deeper than the behaviour, we can't understand why people do the things they do, and we react in fear or misunderstanding.

Under the 'waterline' of our conscious awareness lies the subconscious, the information field where all our life experiences and memories are stored. It is an incredibly sophisticated device which means that, once we have learned a certain skill, we don't have to think about how to do it anymore, it just happens automatically. This is how we drive to work on autopilot each day. It's how we can ride a bike even though the first time we just kept falling off. Once we get the knack of it, it somehow stays. The pattern gets laid down in the subconscious and becomes a kind of behavioural groove that we naturally fall into.

Iceberg model of the mind

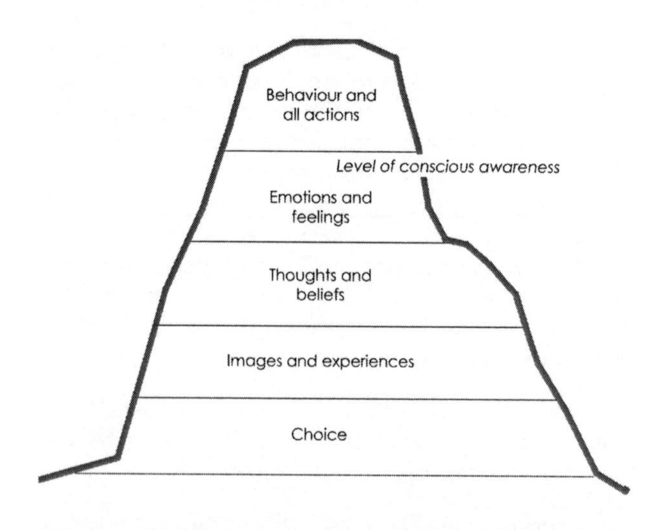

The subconscious also holds all our deeper set thoughts and beliefs learned in childhood about who we are, the way the world works and whether it is kind to us or not. And it holds all the complex, suppressed feelings that accompany those beliefs and thoughts.

For instance, you may rationally know that something like water is nothing to be afraid of. But if you have a phobia of water no amount of rational belief will get you into the swimming pool without feeling some level of fear, or even terror. Hypnotherapists are trained to take you back to the time when this irrational belief was first laid down in the subconscious. There is usually some event, like tripping and falling into a swimming pool that the child-self found frightening or traumatic. At the time, her subconscious mind would have concluded something like: '*Water is dangerous and frightening, therefore I will never go near it again.*'

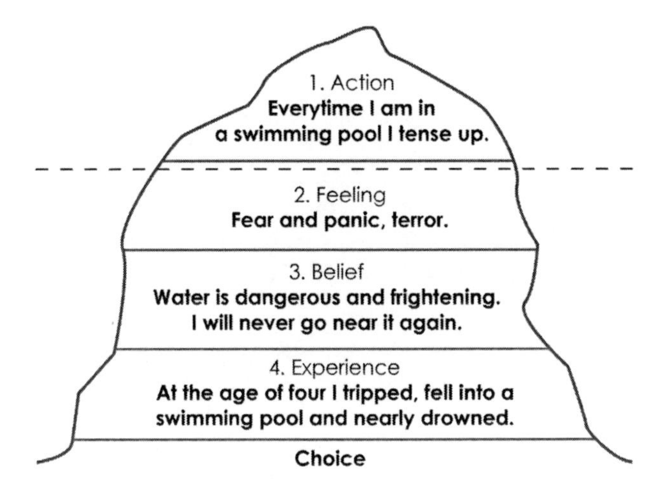

Similarly, when your partner starts acting in a similar way to one of your parents, a way that you found upsetting as a child, it is likely a whole set of emotions sitting in the subconscious get triggered. This is why couples can have full-blown slanging matches over the most trivial events.

Sue says:

Before Jeff and I separated for two years, I used to see a pile of dishes in the sink as the barometer of whether he loved me or not. Was I the doormat here, or did we have a sharing caring relationship? Mostly I just begrudgingly got on with it but there were times when, if Jeff dithered about when it was his turn to pick up the squeezy, I would stomp off in a huff, muttering obscenities under my breath.

In hindsight, applying the iceberg model, underneath my outburst I was feeling unloved and unappreciated. My belief was that despite all the ways I cared for others, they didn't do the same for me. If I go deeper into the layer of experience, I ask myself when I first felt this way; what is the root of this pattern? And I suddenly and vividly remember how, as the eldest of four siblings, I took on looking after the others and felt no one appreciated my efforts, or at least not enough and not in the right way.

The seemingly trivial washing up / housework issue was triggering all the old feelings and beliefs about not being appreciated in my family as a child. Having unearthed the layers underneath my behaviour, I understood that my outbursts were not about Jeff, much as I wanted to pin them on him. Deeper down, the feelings and beliefs came from before I ever met him.

Now as an adult wanting to break free of a pattern I have identified, I can make another choice: the choice to enjoy those times with my sister and brothers, the choice to give myself appreciation and not try to take it from Jeff, expecting him to understand telepathically exactly how and when to give it to me; even the choice to wash up or not. This issue of housework has thankfully disappeared from our relationship, and somehow it all gets done. What a relief!

Situations like this have very little to do with the event itself and everything to do with repressed subconscious feelings being triggered through the mirror of relationship. In our experience, only a very small proportion of any upset is about what is happening in the here and now; although, of course, it may feel very real at the time.

Some years ago Jeff was training a cross-section of people from a large multi-national company in London.

Client Story:

I was teaching the iceberg model and after explaining that our experiences and behaviours come from choices made in our past, I asked the delegates to look at examples of some of their less than attractive behaviours and notice that this was really stuff out of their past.

One of the delegates, a large burly guy called Tom, was clearly attending the training day as part of his job and against his own wishes. When I asked Tom, who was obviously not doing the exercise, how he was finding the seminar, his reply could politely be phrased as: 'Bollocks!' I let it go.

At the next break, as we approached the tea trolley a spider crawled out from under a saucer and this 230 pound guy freaked out. When we returned to the seminar room, I pointed out to him that he had just acted out the model perfectly. Seeing this spider had triggered his fear, and it was obvious that this fear was not something that had started on this day so must have come from his past. He was now willing to go back to an experience in his childhood when he had been frightened by his brother putting spiders in his bed. Tom now understood the mechanism that creates behaviour and incidents in the present. This opened a door to an understanding that gave him more power to change other self-defeating patterns in his life.

We are not born with fears, anger or other poor behaviours. In fact small children often seem fearless. But then things happen and we make choices. Those choices then become our beliefs, then our emotions and finally our behaviours – and we can change all this if we are willing to look just a little deeper at our past experiences and the choices that we made that have such influence in our lives today.

Most of us find it hard to accept that what is upsetting us right now has virtually nothing to do with the present, or that we are not totally aware of every part of our mind. But our work with thousands of clients and workshop participants has shown us that we are hardly ever upset for the reasons we think we are. The characters, film set and story might have changed, but the executive producer (you and your subconscious drives) remains the same.

The other way we like to explain the power of the subconscious is that it functions like a ship sailing on autopilot. You can wake up each morning and set the ship's course north, with a positive affirmation like: *'I will love and accept myself today'*. But as soon as you sleep, it automatically switches direction south and goes back to its subconscious 'default' belief settings like: *'I always get things wrong'* or *'I'm not good enough'*. Subsequently life becomes very difficult, or you don't get anywhere and your conscious mind can't work out why. Despite all your efforts, you stay stuck in your patterns of conflict. Have you noticed yet that your arguments with your partner are all about, essentially, the same issue? Doesn't it feel horribly familiar each time it comes up? Don't the pair of you sound – let's be honest now – like a cracked record?

Not only is your conscious mind flummoxed trying to work out what on earth is going on (apart, of course, from putting the blame squarely on your partner), it can get angry at how downright mean the world is being to you. You may have set great goals in your life, get all fired up to achieve them only to find you fall at the first hurdle. You may have decided you want a loving relationship, but unless your subconscious mind is 'on board' too, it just isn't going to happen. This is what is going on for the people we work with who want a relationship but then, deep down, believe that it is just too scary.

Client Story:

Mary was sitting quietly in a workshop and was obviously in pain. When we asked what was going on she said tearfully how her partner had walked out on her after a five-year relationship. She spent a few minutes speaking of her upset and hurt. Once she was a little more settled we asked her to answer a question with the first thing that came to her mind and not to think about an answer. The question was, 'How come you wanted him to leave?' At first shock registered on her face; then she broke out in a huge smile and said that she was tired of him and wanted to distance herself. People can't help smiling when a subconscious truth is spoken. On the surface it appeared she had lost someone against her will, but in truth she no longer wanted the relationship. Her fear had become too great about moving forward and she wanted out but with a big heartbreak story about how someone had done her so wrong.

Another way that a fear of relationship shows is by choosing to have a relationship with someone who is not really available, falling in love with someone who is already in a relationship or with someone who is not your equal (toy-boys or toy-girls). When you start a relationship like this we call such a person Mr. or Mrs. 80%. Everything looks good but they are not truly available. If you have been out of relationship for a long time and the need becomes so great, you might start an 80% relationship but there is little chance of success: consciously you desire a relationship but what is hidden is the fear of having an equal and significant relationship.

The main thing to remember from this section is that, no matter how much you might pride yourself on your objective, adult, scientific, mature view on life, the universe and everything, the bottom line is that none of us is a rational being – that is, according to the iceberg model, the smallest part of us. We each carry with us a vast subconscious realm of complex choices, memories, thoughts, beliefs and feelings that impact every relationship we enter into, whether that be with our true love or the bloke on the till at the corner shop. Our mental icebergs glide along with us through life, and, just like the one that sank the Titanic, they are a force to be reckoned with. Never, ever, underestimate the power of the subconscious mind.

The Birth of Ego Structure & Behavioural Grooves

In the previous section we looked at how our 'behavioural grooves', like learning to ride a bike, get formed and laid down in the subconscious mind. They become automatic actions that we don't think about, we just do them naturally.

How come some children grow up happy and peaceful, whilst others turn into delinquent knife-wielding hoodies? It is all down to the behavioural grooves that have, through their life experience, been etched into their psyche. Teenagers who hide under their hoods and act out violently are coming from an internalised deep fear for their very survival. They trust no-one and so their aggressive actions automatically kick in as a defence mechanism, in order to, ultimately, keep themselves safe. Such is the strange yet compelling logic of the subconscious mind.

Thankfully most children don't turn out this way. Nevertheless, we all have behavioural grooves that get etched into our psyche in order to survive within the family. It is our natural, child-like way of securing love in the best way our immature subconscious can figure out at the time.

In our childlike naivety we cannot comprehend why one of our parents might suddenly withdraw their affection or yell at us uncontrollably. Children have no frame of reference to put such frightening events into any context. As children, we conclude – subconsciously – that our parents' rage or helplessness must be our fault. We can see no other reason for it.

Client Story:

June attended a workshop in London and became a focus person. She spoke of how much she tried to do everything right in her life and her relationship but how her partner was badly behaved and no matter how she tried she did not feel loved. In an intuitive regression June went back to her childhood when she was woken every night by her parents arguing after she went to bed. When she heard them fighting she felt bad. She couldn't hear what was being said but she remembered that her mother told her often to not be 'naughty' and not to 'drive her mad' by not sharing all her toys with her brother.

June decided on a deep internal level that she was a naughty girl and she must be responsible for her parents' quarrelling. In judging herself, June moved away from her centre and compensated for her bad feelings by taking on the role of 'good girl'. This role helped her to hide the feelings of failure and inadequacy. When she was praised for being a 'good girl' her role was reinforced because June got the approval she wanted, and because she believed she was helping the family.

June's child-like thinking went like this: if I act like a good child I will get love. Once she had made this bargain, June sacrificed herself to pay off the guilt she felt at being the cause of her parents' fights. She created a deep belief that if she had not been born then her parents would not have argued. This is clearly not the truth but is the thinking of a small child whose greatest desire is for her parents' happiness.

June carried this pattern into her marriage. She felt her husband's unhappiness was her fault and then she would fight with her husband about his bad behaviour. She learned that as she tried to hide one aspect of herself, 'naughty person', then she polarised into the 'good one', and he had nowhere else to go but polarise to the opposite and be the 'bad one'.

As June forgave herself and her fighting parents, she was freed of this pattern. She realised that she was not to blame for what happened and had no reason to feel bad. Above all, she understood that sometimes we are good and other times we are not; it is just the way it is.

✓ Try this:

How many behavioural grooves laid down in childhood as a result of various experiences can you identify for yourself? It is not that these are good or bad, and it is not that your parents were good or bad; they were coping with life the best they knew how at the time in whatever circumstances they faced.

Your behavioural grooves arose out of your attempt as a child to secure love for yourself, and to fit in as best you could to what might have been difficult situations. So the only question now is this: If you still find yourself going round and round the same grooves, and if they are blocking your relationships, would you change the record?

- Think of a specific behaviour you would like to change, and then draw a blank iceberg model for yourself.
- At the top write down the action or behaviour, and then intuitively drop down through the layers underneath: first the feelings and emotions associated with it, then the belief that was generated, and finally the original experience.
- There are no right or wrong answers, just relax, be honest with yourself and trust the first answer that pops into your mind, even if it doesn't make sense.
- Finally make a new choice. It is not that the original experience didn't happen, but how could you choose a different response now as an adult looking back at that picture *and everyone else involved?*

To imagine how our perspectives can change, picture yourself standing on top of a hill looking back at your past, your childhood. Some things would be clearly visible from this point of view but also many aspects would be hidden within the deep valleys and forests of your past. If this present moment grew, if this moment became a mountain and you could look back again, you would see your past from a different, higher perspective. You could gain a wider view of what the past was for you, of how things were linked. You can now see more of the topography of your life and see into the valleys and forests of your past.

As we grow in maturity in this present moment we can change how we see our past. We then change how we see ourselves, and we change how we see the future.

Children's Instinctive Drive to 'Help' Their Family

It seems that children have a natural instinct to want to help others.

In America a group of scientists examined the reaction of babies to 'good', 'neutral' and 'bad' wooden toys. In almost all cases, the infants of six to ten months demonstrated a preference for toys that were helpful to others over those which either hindered their progress or 'stood back' and did nothing. In the experiments, babies were shown a display featuring a hill on which were placed wooden block characters with large eyes. A round-shaped character, known as 'the climber', began by resting at the bottom of the hill. After repeated unsuccessful attempts to climb the hill, the climber was either helped to the top by a triangular-shaped 'helper' or pushed back down the hill by a 'bad' square-shaped character. The babies watched the display sitting on the knees of their parents who were instructed not to interfere. After the display, almost all the babies reached out to touch the 'helper' character; they identified themselves most strongly with this character in the story.

Source: Kiley Hamlin, Yale University (Nature, 2007)

It is also well known in child psychology that when the parents' relationship is in trouble, the children often start to act out. If there is a messy divorce, then one child might subconsciously sacrifice himself in a certain way, perhaps by getting sick or having an accident. Another might suddenly get into trouble or start failing at school. All this is a child's instinctive response to somehow help the family by distracting the parents and focusing their attention onto more pressing concerns in the family. They create a drama to stop the parental fighting, at least for a while, and somehow bring the family back together.

It is not hard to find evidence that children who grow up in broken or dysfunctional homes often struggle with life. All children think the woes of their parents are their fault and act accordingly. Naturally, it is easier to see this dynamic in other families than our own, but if the parents' relationship degenerates sufficiently, the children's reactive behaviours will become more extreme: withdrawal, bed-wetting, calling for attention or acting like super good kids. Many 'super good kids' grow up saying they had a perfect childhood, which means they are still living in denial.

✓ Try this:

There is a simple litmus test for whether you grew up having perfect parents and a perfect childhood: it would mean that now you have a great marriage, success beyond your wildest dreams, and kids nearing enlightenment.

If your parents were unhappy, at some deep level you most likely thought it your fault. And, in one way or another, you adapted your behaviours to deal with the guilt and control the situation.

Jeff became the bad apple in the family. Sue was the good child. And both of us carried the guilt of our parents' unhappiness into our relationship. We have all done this, but we can understand our parents from a different perspective, and have the courage to let go of all the past and be ourselves; sometimes good and sometimes bad but always ourselves.

Unless we have resolved or healed the past, we have to bring it into our adult relationships. So here we are today, a ship in full sail with an unexplored iceberg in tow, wondering why we get upset or upset others, trying to navigate the rogue waves of relationships.

Our Original Heartbreak

In their blind love of their parents, without whom they would feel so desperately lost, children will do almost anything to 'save' their family and bring back some kind of harmony. They will do whatever they can to feel loved. This is when those 'fractures in our minds' that we have been talking about come into being. In our childlike confusion, we split off the parts of ourselves that appear to be deemed unacceptable by our parents or society and banish them into the far flung corners of the subconscious. The subconscious says to itself something like: *'I must never act like that again because doing so means I am a bad person who makes my parents do these frightening things.'*

This is our original heartbreak: the shock and pain of realising that our parents cannot fulfill our deepest needs. Cracks form in our bond with our parents and, at the same time, in our relationship with ourselves; we deny and lose a part of who we are. This is where those nagging, underlying feelings of guilt, shame, being worthless, unlovable and not good enough kick in.

Jeff says:

My childhood was heartbreak hotel. Each time I got a hit, part of me did not make it. Having grown up in Africa on a farm, as a teenager I looked tough on the outside, but inside I was a mess. I was a really poor student, painfully withdrawn and slow to make friends. I had the greatest trouble with authority and a severe chip on both shoulders. A poor communicator at best, I could hardly do more than grunt at girls. I had learned to be polite and had good manners and other forms of civilised window dressing but little of my true nature made it out of my childhood.

Needless to say, when it came to relationships it was basically one disaster after another, so being a sailor was perfect for me. I could always find a berth when things started to get sticky, and that typically did not take long. When I first married Sue, it was a sham of a marriage. I was a really poor husband. Away from home, I behaved like a free man. Good looking, polite, independent, adventurous, and fearless on the surface, yet just below I was totally dysfunctional, immature, cowardly and self-interested.

Which one was true? Actually, neither of them. The real me was buried under two conflicting personalities. It has taken a lot of excavation to find those parts that got left behind, but each time I do I find pure gold.

The Other Ninety Percent of You

The needy parts of us can be disowned or repressed but they never disappear completely. Instead, they form sub-personalities in our deeper mind in order to compensate for our perceived inadequacies.

✓ Try this:

Listen closely to the chatter of your mind, the running commentary that plays in the background of your life and you might recognise some of the common sub-personalities. The Inner Critic is the one who can always find harsh words with which to criticise you, no matter what you achieve in life. Other compensatory roles that we take on in order to hide our original, perceived failings include the Achiever (you would be surprised how many millionaire CEOs are driven by deep feelings of failure), the Rebel (a big 'f**k you' reaction), the Martyr (such as mothers who put everyone else's needs before their own) and the Joker (who charms his or her way through life).

The original need for love, safety and true bonding might have been suppressed but it lives on in myriad different roles, all designed to get the original need met. No matter how independent or mature you might think you are, you still have these needs driving you from the subconscious level.

Before we even clap eyes on our true love, we have amassed one big iceberg of subconscious needs, desires and emotional complexes. This subconscious world makes up about 90 percent of our mind, according to the iceberg model. Yet, mostly, we are oblivious to it. Much of it is repressed and much of it happens automatically in reaction to others. Look at those terrible road rage incidents. It's not the actual event that causes such over-reactions but the feelings of powerlessness and rage it triggers in the mind of the guy who shouts obscenities at the unsuspecting driver who cut him up at the lights.

Many of us suspect that we are sitting on some kind of volcano but we don't feel we have the tools or know-how to deal with such issues, so our instinct is to keep them buried... and then we start a relationship!

Jeff says:

When I was young and provoked, I would erupt into violence. As I grew older and wiser I would emit cold fury. Now I can feel the rage coming like a gigantic locomotive thundering directly towards its target, but I recognise it and have time to make other choices. I also know it is in my best interest to make different choices *and* quickly. The cost of being in reaction to these powerful and often destructive emotions is painfully familiar to me.

Most of us keep these emotions deeply hidden. It is, however, in our best interests to deal with them at some point because if we don't, they will work away at us affecting our health and general well being. These emotions can be dealt with and transformed, they can be changed from destructive to creative but you must feel them first, and grow enough in maturity and wisdom so you can handle such power.

✓ Try this:

Think back to the last time you felt either anger or rage. Did you bury it or did you act it out? Was it cold, remote fury or was it the volcano?

Who was there with you? Notice that when you get angry there is always someone else there.

Whatever happened in that incident that came to mind, how distant from the other person or people did you feel afterwards? Then, can you acknowledge that 'this is me. I get angry'. Because to deny it is to repress it and when you repress or deny this so very human part of yourself, that makes you dangerous.

Finally, imagine that you can feel the anger without imposing it on the people around you, without blaming anyone else even though they are triggering it within you. Various therapies suggest walking, hitting pillows, going outside and yelling to let off steam, counting to ten, taking deep breaths. Or you could just feel it until it changes.

Jeff says:

Many years into my training it was possible for me to sit in a chair and feel anger and even rage without having to act it out. This was a great step forward for me and certainly made the lives of the people around me easier. By then, I recognised that I frequently offloaded my stress by becoming angry, which was a really poor strategy. I saw that when I became angry I make the whole universe about me. All the other people in my life may as well be walking around with a paper bag on their heads.

Lastly, I realised when I felt anger it was because I believed someone, usually Sue, had deprived me of something. But with a quick look at the dynamics I soon saw it was me that was depriving myself. And the thing that I felt deprived of, I was actually scared of having, which was a bummer when it came to sex. However, while we certainly did have our fights over sex, the thing that seemed to press our buttons the most was discussions over money. We have transcended most of the issues in this area now, basically because I leave it all up to Sue. Even in a good marriage or partnership there is usually one area that brings up our unresolved anger and sex and money are prime triggers.

If we believe we are dangerous, that our anger can explode at random, we will push others away and distance ourselves from the people we love the most. It is as if deep inside we feel like a suicide bomber but because we don't really want to hurt anyone, we cover up and withdraw. This comes at a huge cost to ourselves, and to our relationships with our families and our friends.

✓ Try this:

As a percentage, how much have you withdrawn from the people around you, and from life?

Do you fear your own reactions, or do you worry more about other people's reactions?

Whatever your answers, how much would you like to find a better way?

Relationships: Your Magic Mirror

In Buddhist philosophy there is a saying that although we can see others, we cannot see ourselves. The place where all these subconscious needs, drives and emotional complexes really come to light are in what we call the 'magic mirror of relationship.'

On our own we are, quite literally, blind to our subconscious drives. We live in reaction to others and blame them for making us feel that way (such as Mr Road Rage). But in a close, committed, loving relationship we simply cannot avoid it. All those subconscious drives and frozen pockets of pain will come up into the light for healing. It is absolutely unavoidable.

Many marriages and relationships have foundered on the ignorance of the principle that our partners are our mirrors. Unless we become willing to research this dynamic we will stay distant from, if not in full-scale warfare with, our nearest and dearest. Only by understanding this, can we pave a path to happiness and marital bliss (even if it is only for a few moments at a time!).

Jeff says:

One of my major issues with Sue was that she was not courageous enough; in fact she lived in fear. Now I had been a tough sailor; fear was not a word I had in my vocabulary. It would drive me nuts when she was so cautious and I would attack her for it. But when I got honest and recognised how I had repressed my inner fear, especially around emotions and intimacy, I was firstly shocked, then humbled. Once I owned my own fear and then moved back towards Sue we put the whole issue behind us.

✓ Try this:

When we are counselling couples that are just about to split up, this exercise is often our first port of call.

First, ask yourself the question, 'What pisses me off so much about my partner?' Then the second question is, 'Do you recognise that once you acted in exactly the same way?' and the usual answer is 'Never!'

Any strong emotion associated with a behaviour in your partner is always a sure sign of buried and repressed issues. Otherwise you would not be upset and ready to hit the road.

Now, it is just a matter of honesty and choice. You can continue to be right about your partner and stay fighting or you can acknowledge your own past behaviour that you have tried to keep hidden.

> With an ounce of courage you can take the first step back to a functional relationship by forgiving your partner for what they are doing, because at the same time what you are really doing is forgiving yourself for your past. Then join them in love and honest communication.

When you are willing to think of your partner as your mirror, as your portal to looking at your darker parts and the emotions around when you started to believe you were the same in some way, your relationships will switch from hell to heaven. Suddenly you will glimpse a way through the minefield.

Who Are You Without Your Behavioural Grooves?

Without all the drama in your life, without the fights over those discarded toenail clippings or whatever it is your partner does that drives you completely insane, who are you really? Are you this identity, your role as a husband or wife, your lurking subconscious complexes of needs and repressed emotions? Or are you, in essence, something deeper and more profound than all of that? Behind every mask you wear, every persona you adopt for the outside world, who are you really? Who were you, for example, when you were a tiny baby?

Even the most hardened skeptic who balks at the very mention of the word 'spiritual' or 'energy' has to work very hard not to melt when looking into a baby's eyes. A baby's eyes hold a sense of innocence and wonder that bring us into the deep mystery of what it is to be human. Being around little children who are so fully in the present moment, with all their glee and love of life, can be such a tonic when we are weary with our own incessant thoughts and judgments about how bad life, or that partner of ours, can be. Let's just call this state of childlike innocence, this place beyond the judging mind, your original shining light.

Adapted Ego Structure or Shining Light?

As the child grows up, the ego structure starts getting formed around this shining light. A baby with good bonding with his mother initially doesn't know that he is a separate being, he is still umbilically attached. Once it dawns on the infant that he is a separate individual, he starts experimenting with his own sense of personal power, by saying 'no' – to pretty much everything. Parents who have survived the 'terrible twos' stage will testify to this. And so the child's little ego structure begins forming, ideally into a healthy sense of identity with strong boundaries and a good level of self-love so that he can enjoy healthy, loving relationships later in life.

But what if the child's upbringing wasn't ideal? Then the ego structure starts getting a bit – how shall we put it? – wonky. It has to adapt in order to survive and secure the love and attention all children crave.

Imagine your psychological structure like a building. First you need good, solid foundations on which to build a sustainable structure that will stand the test of time. If a baby was neglected, he would make choices and his subconscious might have already programmed beliefs like: *'My parents ignore me when I cry, therefore my needs are not important.'* Or even: *'I obviously don't exist. I might as well never bother asking for help from anyone.'* Beliefs like this are not good foundations for a healthy ego. Wobbly foundations mean that the rest of the ego structure isn't going to be too stable either.

If you subconsciously and pre-verbally concluded you might as well never bother asking for help from anyone, then you could become a loner and disappear into your own world for hours at a time. This could be where a child develops an extraordinary imagination, but it is also a deeply lonely place, where it is difficult to connect with others and feel their affections.

If the foundations aren't stable, then as our ego structure builds throughout childhood, we have to create strange and elaborate formations within our building in order to compensate for the early weaknesses in its basic structure. Dodgy DIY patch-up jobs paper over the cracks of our uniquely skewed psyche. You might even build some elaborate system of ropes and pulleys to keep it all together. All this takes up emotional energy that will hold you back later in life; it is frozen pain awkwardly held together within the adapted ego structure.

Client Story:

Ellen was consistently put down and undermined as a child, so she developed an arrogant front to hide her deep insecurities about her self-worth. Her structure was particularly unsustainable, so it was vulnerable to collapse later in life. In fact, she had a nervous breakdown, which happens when keeping up the front becomes too exhausting. Ellen was propelled back into those original feelings of undermined self-worth, in order to feel and process them properly with help and understanding. She could then rebuild her whole inner ego structure into something more sustainable and true to herself.

Projection

Our masks, personas and ego defences surround and hide our original shining light. We don't see the world as it really is; as incredibly beautiful and full of wonder as it was to us when we were a newborn baby. All that wonder hasn't gone anywhere; it is still inside us. We don't need to learn anything new or be any different to discover it again. We simply need to recognise and understand the skewed ego-structure that has obscured it.

This light then starts casting strangely shaped shadows; all the adapted ego structure, all those roles we take on to compensate for our original perceived failings, become shadow projected onto the people around us. We see the world through the limitations and shadows of our minds. Let's just hold that image of our ego structure casting shadows onto others for a moment; we will need it as we move into the next part of this book and learn what, exactly, is going on throughout all the stages of relationships.

From this vantage point, we can see that our uniquely adapted ego structure has been created to help us navigate and survive in the world we grew up in. As adults, the structure has become so well-formed, so deeply entrenched in the behavioural grooves of our psyche that, to us, it is absolutely real. It colours every aspect of our lives; and dictates not only how we 'do' relationships but how we 'do' everything. Yes, it feels as real as the chair you are presumably sitting on. But is it really the true you?

Love Breaks Your Heart Open

True love – and we are talking about the larger, universal state of love – will eventually, if we dare surrender to it, melt all the frozen pain held in your adapted, skewed ego structure. Love touches us deep inside, it reaches the parts of us we had no idea even existed, it moves us like nothing else can – and it takes no prisoners. Everything – and we mean *everything* – that is broken in our minds; every unfelt hurt, every unmet need will show up in the glare of its light. Nothing can hide from it. True love will shine its light on everything unlike itself, in order for it to be seen, resolved and healed.

When our adapted ego structure starts crumbling, when the frozen pockets of pain have been touched and melted by love, then it feels like our heart is breaking. Your heart doesn't just break when someone you adore dumps you. It breaks time and time again within a long-term relationship. True love is not about making you happy in the short term. It is about breaking your heart wide, wide open – so your untrue structure can melt and so that you can return to your source of wonder once more.

In our experience, a 'big love' exists way beyond romantic love. Some people call it oneness, others say it is divine, others wrap it up in religious terminology. We call it by different names and feel it in different ways - in the presence of a beautiful sunset, holding a baby, reading an inspirational book, or when someone totally believes in us. But in each case, someone - or something - sneaks past our defences and overpowers us with feelings of love, of gratitude, of appreciation, of compassion. In that moment, we are laid bare with feelings that take us as far as, but in the opposite direction of, our rage.

In our seminars we witness huge acts of courage and humanity. When those waves of love and compassion break through it is a moment of grace that changes us forever. No matter what else happens in our lives that reality is always within us. That love is around us in a thousand ways every single day and all we need to do is to have the courage to open to it, to stand vulnerable before life, before nature and if we truly do that it will sweep us away.

We believe that falling in love is one of the ways that we humans can access this blissful state but in order to stay connected to that bigger love, our relationship invites us to work through every inner obstacle that obscures our view of it. And the perfect place to do this is within your relationship. The path of true love, as they say, never did run smooth. But it is worth every stumble, trip, dead end, false start and detour, if it gets us back to that place of innocence.

Jeff says:

When I think back on my past and dwell on the people who continued to believe in me, I feel great appreciation. Allowing the love of others to reach in and touch me keeps my heart open.

I can remember a moment after 20 years of marriage when I looked at Sue lying on the bed and I was overwhelmed by her magnificence. My perception of her went far beyond her physical body. It was as if I saw her for the first time. I have experienced these moments of great love for my children, moments of understanding that I can only describe as angelic. And even those, oh so rare moments of love that wash me to pieces that can only come from the source of love.

And all because I had the willingness to open myself up, and each experience makes it so much easier to keep going.

From Blame to Responsibility

Ultimately, we are all innocent. And, yes, we believe this includes our parents, carers and other adults who were instrumental in our childhood psychological development, damaging or otherwise.

> **Try this:**
>
> This may be a big leap of understanding for you, especially if the home you grew up in was particularly harsh or neglectful. You may be feeling a reluctance to forgive or see through your carer's eyes. This is understandable. But if you resist, you are only perpetuating that hurt by bringing it into your own relationships.
>
> So isn't it worth it to start looking at forgiveness? Do you see how it can free you to live fully?

We can start to accept that our parents did the best they could with the inner resources they had at the time. They did their best – just as we know we have done if we are parents – and, of course, they could have done better. But, until we are able to truly stand in their shoes, feel their inner turmoil and see the world through their eyes, who are we to judge them as bad, wrong or guilty of heinous crimes against us? It is a common trap to fall into; the yearning that if only things had been better in our childhoods, then maybe we wouldn't struggle so much in life or have such trouble within our relationships.

Forgiveness certainly isn't about condoning abuse or taking some kind of superior, moral high ground and magnanimously letting guilty parties off the hook. True, someone significant might have made a mistake and hurt us long ago in our lives. But by not forgiving we are still caught in the problem; and we will also find it hard to forgive ourselves for the mistakes we have and will inevitably make. Forgiving is about acknowledging and feeling our pain in order to let it go and be free to 'give forth' of ourselves again. When we do that, when we let go of feeling sorry for ourselves and blaming others for our problems, then we have a chance to move forward in life. And when we move forward, we find success in all its forms: work, finance, love, friendships. Success in the widest sense of the word is the product of a joyful life, not the cause of it.

In fact we can blame those who have perpetrated against us all we like, but the responsibility for our feelings and reactions to them and others, remains ours alone. Apart from saying sorry (which, of course, can be wonderful to hear) there is little they can do to change our inner programming and the skewed ego structure we have been left with. Only we can do that. It is one of the great challenges of life.

It had to get really bad for us before we were willing to look at things in a different way, and start to take responsibility for our behaviour. The turning point in our marriage came when we stopped blaming each other. Instead of thinking of each other as the worst mistake of our lives, we switched the telephoto lens to a wider view: we were each in this relationship for a reason, with bad feelings that started long before we met each other, and we might as well learn the lessons, instead of tearing each other apart.

It is our job to take responsibility for our lives, our problems and our troubled relationships. Tools like positive or behavioural psychology and repeating affirmative mantras help with the symptoms, but they don't get right in there and sort out the causes. Similarly, talking for years with an analyst about your terrible childhood can keep you stuck in the self-pity loop too. We offer a different approach, one that addresses the feelings and the deeply-set subconscious roots of issues that come up in relationships. One that recognises that these very issues can *expand* us, rather than define us, can propel us forward in life if we have the courage to face them head on.

But first, let's take a look at the hidden dynamics at play between you and your beloved. In Part Two we are going to take you on a tour of the stages that relationships go through – and tell you our story. We have been there. We have made many, many mistakes and we want to show you what we have learned.

Part Two:

THE STAGES OF RELATIONSHIPS

'Life does not consist mainly, or even largely, of facts and happenings. It consists mainly of the storm of thought that is forever flowing through one's head.'

Mark Twain

All relationships evolve through stages on the way to partnership. You know when you have reached partnership with someone when you feel you are both on the same team; each of you accepts and values the other for who they are and each of you contributes your talents to the partnership. There is closeness, balance and a feeling of peace and optimism that, together, you can deal with any challenge life throws at you. You no longer worry that the relationship might be over every time you disagree.

The closer the relationship, the more steps we encounter on our way to partnership. We know we are faced with another step when we have an emotional reaction of some kind. Will we act out in the same old way or will we make a change? Committed relationships are a journey, not a destination. They evolve and require each partner to continuously evolve too. If we do not learn from and work on our relationships, then our relationships will not work.

Below is an outline of the stages that all relationships go through. We have made the stages as chronological as we can but, by their very nature, relationships don't all follow an exact formula. They do, however, display similar patterns and dynamics, which we are sure you will recognise.

1. Honeymoon (or Romance) Stage

2. Power Struggle Stage

    The Shadow
    The Dependent-Independent Dance
    Polarisation
    The Six Dynamics of Fighting

3. Dead Zone Stage

    Roles, Rule, Duties & Fusion
    Family Dynamics, Sacrifice & Indulgence
    Competition
    Fear of the Next Step

4. Partnership Stage

Are you ready? Let's take a deep breath and jump in.

Chapter 4

THE HONEYMOON

> *'Why do birds suddenly appear, every time you are near? Just like me, they want to be close to you.'*
>
> **The Carpenters**

Falling in love is undoubtedly one of nature's greatest 'highs'. The prolific spiritual author Dr Deepak Chopra goes so far as to say that it is 'the most powerful spiritual experience most of us will have in our lifetimes.' Why? Because it brings out the best – the 'shining light' – in both of you.

Even if it is only for a short time, being in love transports you into that magical reality of your original innocent baby state, where everything is new and a source of endless wonder. The birds are singing, the sky is blue... or maybe it is raining, in which case you skip along, splashing in the puddles, getting soaked and loving every minute. You might stare dreamily out of the bus window, and become transfixed at the sight of a tiny raindrop trickle down the glass. The most mundane, ordinary things suddenly become extraordinarily beautiful. It is the best feeling and, of course, we want it to last forever.

So what causes such a heady rush? How come only this particular person can make you feel this way?

In the movie 'Sleepless in Seattle', the female lead Annie (Meg Ryan) asks her psychoanalyst friend Dennis (David Hyde Pierce) about how he fell in love with his wife:

Annie: *'But when you first met her, did you know that she was the only one for you – that in some kind of mystical, cosmic way it was fated?'*

Dennis: *'Annie, when we're attracted to someone it just means that your subconscious is attracted to their subconscious, subconsciously. So what we think of as fate is really just two neuroses knowing they're a perfect match.'*

As we've already established, our subconscious makes up 90 per cent of who we are. It is what actually drives the bulk of our behaviour – whether we are aware of it or not. Sure, your new love might look like the real deal, have all the bumps in the right places, but it's their subconscious *presence* in the room that attracts you to them like a magnet, like two tuning forks resonating together at the same frequency. Your level or type of repressed pain and needs are 'singing' with theirs. You match, click, resonate; you're on the same wavelength. At some point you may even start 'making sweet music' together.

The other way we describe this mysterious attraction is by saying two people have 'chemistry'. Leading 'love scientist', the biological anthropologist and research professor Dr Helen Fisher, says that being in love produces the same effect on the brain as the rush of being high on cocaine. The same bio-chemicals are involved. Just by meeting this one person, you become, quite literally, intoxicated. But *why* that particular person lights your fire and rings your bell by a single glance in your direction, is still being discussed. Until the power of the subconscious is fully understood (and how do you measure that scientifically?), the biochemical changes involved are but one part of the full picture.

At Last! Someone to Meet Our Original Needs

When you fall in love, you think that your prince or your princess has arrived in your life. But actually, it is your 'button pusher' that has arrived. Except you don't realise it – yet. In fact, how good you feel being reunited with this missing piece of yourself, tells you how hurt you were to lose it in the first place. In order to get back to wholeness, to your original innocent state, you will have to go back through all the pain that caused you to be so 'heartbroken' in the first place.

The honeymoon stage is a short stage, rarely longer than a year and often much shorter. It shows the potential you have as a couple and acts like glue, creating the bond that will keep you together through the tough times.

When you are head over heels in love, high as a kite, bursting with joy, of course you want it to last forever. It looks and feels like true love, but (and we are sorry to disappoint you here) that is not what is going on. If it were, it would last forever, right? And you would live happily ever after, wouldn't you? But very, very few relationships turn out that way. The very nature of honeymoons is that they do not last.

What we think is love, is, in fact, how we would feel all the time if all our emotional needs for attention, love, nurturing and understanding were being met at any moment in time. It is what we have yearned for deeply since childhood. When we fall in love it finally feels like all those early needs are being taken care of. You might get flowers, love notes and other romantic surprises. You become carefree and do spontaneous, silly things together, like children who just want to play all day. It feels like heaven on earth – and in many ways it is.

If we had had all our needs taken care of in our original family, then we would have grown up feeling like this all the time – about everyone and everything. It is our original 'innocent' state.

Positive Projection

When we fall in love, we are *positively* projecting onto the object of our affections (rather than negatively projecting onto them, which comes later). We are projecting everything we know to be good about ourselves, our own 'shining light', onto our partner – and because we love it about ourselves and see it in them, we then believe that we love them.

Often, our friends will question this glowing picture we paint of our newfound sweetheart. There is a saying that love is blind, and this is why: we don't truly see our new partner. We just see the positive projections. Meanwhile, our friends might be blinded (or at least partially sighted) due to their own negative projections.

Every one of us has probably had an experience when a friend has fallen in love and has described their new partner in the most positive way. They might even offer to introduce us to them, which mostly out of kindness we accept, imagining we are going to meet Prince or Princess Charming. When we meet them it is hard to keep a straight face as they appear to be very different from how they have been portrayed.

It's important that you don't try and put your friend straight about their new partner. If you do, you will stand accused of wanting to destroy the most beautiful thing that ever happened to them. They see in their new partner everything good they actually believe about themselves. You, in turn, will view their partner through your own set of projections. We see everyone around us through the filters of our mind, so what is the truth? Well, that depends who is asking and who is looking.

Jeff says:

My biggest test came about with our daughter's first significant relationship. One look at him and every negative thing I could imagine came up for me and yet she embraced him as the love of her life. I was caught between wanting to support and understand my daughter and throwing her boyfriend headlong out of the house with dire warnings about what would happen if he ever returned.

I realised I was at a choice point. Either I could plot abduction by the French Foreign Legion, which would inevitably lead to a fight with our daughter, or I could start to deal with some of my own projections. I quickly realised much of what I thought about him and his behaviour was based on how I had treated girlfriends in my late teens. It wasn't easy, but I got to the point of being polite and accepting. At about which time our daughter emerged from the honeymoon stage and started to see him in a negative light. Shortly after she threw him out!

No Relationship Starts for the Right Reasons

As we have said, contrary to popular belief, the honeymoon stage is *not* based on love. It is based on the belief that someone (our rescuing prince or princess), can fulfill all our needs. When we are in love, we feel like we are wrapped up in a soft, warm, fuzzy blanket of total care and protection (the kind of care we always wanted from our parents.) Our positive projections elevate our soulmate from being an ordinary, fallible human being, to a super-human love-machine who can save us from pain and despair. Ooops. That is one big load of expectations to lay on someone that you supposedly 'love'. How can we possibly see them for who they really are at this stage?

This is why the honeymoon stage does not last. It is an illusion – and it is only a matter of time before the illusion starts to disintegrate, right in front of our eyes.

Some couples in long term relationships become so jaded that they forget they ever had a honeymoon – but all relationships start here. At the beginning, we love that our partner is different from us. We love those cosy intimate chats about life, the universe and everything; we are fascinated by their views on politics, culture and religion. But as the honeymoon fades, we start getting upset by these differences. Sooner or later, we will move into the power struggle stage and start to fight about who takes care of whose needs in the relationship.

Naturally when we are in our honeymoon stage we think ours is different and ours is unique and ours will survive but no-one escapes this stage because all relationships always start for the wrong reasons. Eventually we will come to a decision point when the honeymoon ends and we can either believe that is the end of the relationship or we can make the decision to understand what is really going on. It dawns on us that our partner is our mirror, reflecting back to us the personal issues that we need to work on. Love relationships are, basically, about bringing our shadow selves into the light of awareness. Once we have put the inner work in, once we have cleaned up our act enough to see our partner for who they really are, then we can make the relationship for the right reason: for love.

OUR STORY: How We Met and Fell in Love

We met in 1974 and married in 1979 when Sue was pregnant with our first child.

Sue says:

Meeting Jeff for the first time was so romantic. I was in recovery from my first marriage and doing up an old wooden boat in Ibiza at the time, and a friend of mine roped me into crewing on this yacht race from Cowes to Cork, at the last minute. I joined the crew in Cowes after flying to the UK,and there was Jeff, the handsome, rugged, live-aboard skipper.

Clapping eyes on Jeff was like a heart-stopping scene from a Mills and Boon novel – the chemistry was there between us immediately. It felt like we spent the entire time on board making eyes at each other and, for me, it was dizzying. All my senses were heightened, constantly on the alert for the next sign of flirtation. I had been married before, but this felt like being a shy teenager again. Living aboard a 50 foot racing yacht with ten others meant there was no chance to be alone together for two weeks, which only added to the tension and all those tantalising 'Does he? Doesn't he?' moments as we shot glances at each other. As soon as we were ashore, our romance began in earnest.

The honeymoon period lasted for about three months while we worked together on the boat and sailed it to Gibraltar, but once I got back to the UK I got cold feet about how this hunky sailor would fit into my hectic London life in educational publishing. I was involved in media initiatives – at one point I was part of a team bidding for the first London commercial radio station – and I was almost embarrassed to introduce Jeff to my friends. After the honeymoon the differences were showing up; me the city sophisticate, Jeff the wild blue yonder maverick, and it seemed impossible to reconcile them. So I pulled back for a while and things were quite rocky between us.

Jeff says:

When I met Sue she was everything I wanted – beautiful, funny and she even owned an old boat in the Mediterranean. At the time, I was living on a friend's racing yacht on the Solent and was asked to help a group of sailors sail it in an Ocean Race to Ireland. We started the yacht race from Cowes, heading out past The Needles into the teeth of a Force 9 gale, and fell in love over a heaving mass of water and ten other sea-sick fellow sailors. The attraction between us was obvious to everyone on board, but there was little we could do about it until we hit dry land.

We quickly made up for lost time and were soon honeymooning together in Ibiza for three months, while working on Sue's boat. Being with Sue felt like a dream come true. We lived and worked in complete harmony, paying attention to every nuance of each other's needs. We spent warm, balmy evenings in small Spanish

> restaurants and loving nights back in our small rented farmhouse. Once the boat was seaworthy, we sailed to Gibraltar with two friends. But then it ended with a bit of a crash when Sue got back to London and had second thoughts – and we said goodbye to our honeymoon stage for a long time. After Sue left I was heartbroken. It had been such a whirlwind romance and now she was gone. I did understand she had to go back but our goodbye was brief and already distant and I knew she was returning to her former life in London. I started drinking heavily and looked for another relationship as I headed out on my next yacht delivery. We were not in touch until I returned to the UK several months later.

Our honeymoon period is the carrot not the stick of relationships. The honeymoon stage is based on illusion but it does have several good aspects and indicators.

Firstly it gets people into relationships. Speaking with couples that have become caught in an unfulfilled relationship, we find that some will swear blind that they never had a honeymoon. 'I never loved him/her!' is a popular refrain. This just shows how buried the good moments of the relationship are. We all had a honeymoon, even if it was very short. It's how all our relationships started.

Secondly the honeymoon stage is indicative of the potential of the relationship. As good as it appears to be in the honeymoon stage, is as good as the relationship will be continuously once we have done our work.

The honeymoon can also act as a great motivator. Each time we work through an issue with our partner we get another honeymoon phase and, as we tell our seminar participants, when you hit the honeymoon head for the nearest hotel to celebrate. Don't delay! It's likely that by the following week a new issue will have come to the surface and you will be back down the pit again.

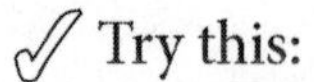

Think back to your last honeymoon period, when you felt in love, happy, carefree and on a cloud. Would you like to go back there?

You can now by imagining yourself in that scene with all the feelings and emotions of the honeymoon. Taste how delicious it was. Now ask yourself, which do you want? That honeymoon or what you have now? It is your choice!

Chapter 5

THE POWER STRUGGLE STAGE

'Now you've got the best of me, come on and take the rest of me, oh baby.'

Billy Ocean

There is a scene in an episode of the American sitcom 'Will & Grace' when one of Will's gay friends announces that he has a new boyfriend. *'Oh I am so excited,'* he exclaims, bouncing up and down with glee, *'I have already booked us in for couples' counselling!'* The fact is, having done such a great job reflecting back to us all our wonderful, positive qualities, our dreamboat will, eventually, start reflecting back to us all the negative stuff too; all the skewed ego structure, all the masks and defence mechanisms we have unwittingly built up around our original 'shining light.'

In many ways, falling in love is like two lost souls in a forest whooping with joy to find each other... only to later realise that they are now both lost together. But hey, we all do it. As we have said before, no-one ever marries for the right reasons. Whereas love is supposed to be about giving unconditionally to the object of our affections, we are all, in fact, secretly 'on the take.' The bottom line is we are all just trying to get our needs met, needs that were set up in childhood, long before we ever met our partner.

As the honeymoon fades, all our partner's strange habits and foibles that we once found endearing now start irritating us. The power struggle begins and the fights start creeping in, as the fractures in our minds start coming to the surface. It is like our relationship draws them out of us so we can take a good look at them, resolve them and move on.

It looks like your partner has changed. *'This is not the person I fell in love with'* you might say to yourself, indignantly. The brutal fact is that what we love about each other at first – what magnetically attracts us to our mate – later turns out to be what we start hating about them. Ouch.

OUR STORY: The Roots of Our Power Struggle

Sue says:

I am the eldest of four children and was often asked to keep an eye on my younger brothers and sister. I remember taking it on myself to amuse them for what seemed like hours on Sunday mornings, so my parents could have a lie-in. I got lots of approval every time I was responsible; it felt like a surefire way to be loved. My father was a staunch Quaker and a civil servant, the archetypal 'Mr Responsible.' In order to keep his approval there was no way I could act irresponsibly. In fact, any member of our family who did act irresponsibly got punished, mostly by cold silent disapproval, being grounded or having pocket money confiscated. It set up a lot of competition and strong family patterns around responsibility – and I became the bossy one. By the time I entered my late teens I was 'Ms Responsible' personified. It was one of the driving forces of my life.

Jeff says:

I am the second of three sons born within three years of each other. Our little sister came along eight years later. My irresponsible behaviour is legendary in the family; we laugh now trying to count the number of cars I wrote off, the number of anniversaries I missed and so on. I grew up on a farm in Africa into a family which thought it had fled its own family dynamics by going to the colonies – only to repeat all these dynamics, of course. My older brother grew up to be the responsible one, so for me the choice was either to become more responsible than him or to become the wild one. In this case, I became the wild one and made life hell for everyone around me. While there were moments of conformity, the underlying pattern was to distance myself and forsake any responsibility.

At the age of 13 my mother, brothers and sister left for Australia as the family was emigrating, leaving me – too much of a handful for my mother – and my father in Africa to complete the sale of our farm. For most of that year I was either safely out of the way in boarding school in Nairobi, or alone on the family farm in west Kenya. The boarding school regime was tough and humiliating, so I became emotionally distant in order to survive. I had little concern for other people and their feelings – I was, after all, so distant from my own feelings. I believed I had built myself into a strong, fearless, independent being. And this was the pattern I brought into my relationship with Sue.

Can you see where this is going? It was years before we even had an inkling of why, after the initial attraction, this responsible-irresponsible issue became the central dynamic of our fights. We each, of course, put the blame squarely on the other. Having been attracted by Jeff's free-wheeling adventurousness, Sue now found Jeff's carelessness infuriating; whilst Jeff, at first loving Sue's steadiness, now found her attention to detail unbearably restricting.

> It felt very, very real at the time, but it is obvious to us now that neither of us were actually upset for the reasons we thought we were. We were like two dogs fighting over some bit of old rag, each with locked jaws, growling and pulling with all their might, using up a lot of emotional energy and getting nowhere fast. We were both hell-bent on trying to change each other into who we each thought the other should be. We both truly believed that we were right; that only when the other changed, would we be happy. What a huge mistake.

When we become adults, fall in love and get married, it is easy to think that we have left all the drama and insecurities of our childhood behind. We may have taken the decision early on that we would never, ever repeat the patterns we see in our parents' relationship. But there they are, smack bang in front of us, in our own relationship. It looks like cracks are forming in our bond with our partner. But this isn't the end of the story – it is just the beginning. As we take responsibility for ourselves and transform our relationship issues, then the whole thing moves upwards like a spiral. Every time we come back into harmony with our partner, the reward is we get to have another honeymoon with them.

Try this:

Very occasionally we meet a couple who say that they have never had a fight or power struggle in their relationship. In our experience this is because they have never really got close to each other, never closed the gap enough between them; the rest of us fight.

In any fight you are being right about something and typically the extent to which you are being right, your partner will be right in the opposite direction. Both of you are being right because you don't want to feel a bad feeling and that feeling at its deepest is always the same feeling in both people. The deepest feeling could be a fear of being abandoned or rejected, a sense of not being valued, some self-hatred, or anything else we fight not to feel.

Remember, in a relationship you have a choice about being right or being happy. Think of a power struggle you are in with your partner or if you don't have a current partner think about an ex partner.

What are you being right about? Think of the last fight you had, or maybe the last fight you avoided. What was it you felt so strongly about?

Can you see that whatever you felt so strongly about was not only to do with the present situation? Can you trace the link to when you felt the same at some point in your past, with your original family, over an event at school or with childhood friends?

Power Struggle Stage Trap 1. The Shadow

As we come out of the honeymoon stage, the first pitfall many of us have to navigate, is when our partner starts to develop some behaviour that we had never seen before. We call this the shadow stage and it goes something like this: If we have a pet hate or strong judgement about others' behaviour – for example, we just can't bear 'lazy' people or 'arrogant' people – then, to our horror, our partner starts, apparently, acting out those very same qualities that we just can't stand.

 Client Story:

Sofia complained that there were no decent men around. She was a cultured, educated, society woman who loved to entertain well and expected her partner to have impeccable manners. She told me she had experienced three significant relationships in the last twelve years. At the outset, each man had seemed to be a perfect gentleman. Within a short space of time, however, each developed the most appalling table manners; belching, farting and eating with their hands rather than the exquisite array of silver cutlery. After trying and failing to change their behaviour, she ended each relationship.

I pointed out to her that there were two common denominators here; all the situations involved bad manners and they all involved her. It transpired that at the age of 12 she had been sitting at the family dining table playing with her food. Her father, sitting nearby, had just come from a business meeting where he had been told about a serious reversal in his fortunes. He was overwhelmed with stress and, at one point, slapped his daughter on her hand and yelled at her to stop playing with her food.

She adored her father and so, at that point, subconsciously blamed herself for his anger. She made an inner promise to 'never be bad-mannered again', and repressed that part of herself. Once her adult love relationships reached the power struggle stage, her partners inevitably acted out her 'bad-mannered' self on her behalf.

This perfectly illustrates how our 'true love' can start looking like our worst nightmare in an alarmingly short space of time. Aghast at what is happening, we start making that most basic of relationship mistakes: we start trying to change our partner. Indignantly, we become right about something – and that means we make our partner wrong. The relationship starts polarising into a 'good cop, bad cop' scenario in our minds.

Of course, what we are doing with our partner we are also doing with our community, our society, and the world around us. We even make the whole of the opposite sex wrong with sweeping statements like: 'All men are bastards,' or: 'You can never trust a woman.' But once we integrate our shadows through the mirror of our relationship we can then move outward, like ripples in a pond, to integrate our wider shadows.

Once Sofia had found the root cause of her behaviour she could change the pattern. Each time her partner acted out the bad mannered part of herself, at one level she reacted as a 12 year-old, traumatised girl; part of her had never grown up past this incident, and every instance of bad manners triggered the pain of the original incident, reinforcing her belief about her partners' behaviours. In a role-play healing exercise she forgave her father and herself and re-integrated the 12 year-old girl, healing that fracture in her mind.

Sofia went on into her next relationship and later married and now has children. There are still moments of bad manners but now she responds as a mature woman and is able to communicate with her husband and children about her feelings and experiences without blame or control. She reports that incidents of bad manners are now very few and far between.

Many relationships do not withstand a strong shadow trap, which is why some of the most passionate relationships fall apart soon after the honeymoon stage. People who have a whole list of 'shadow' issues, which become their relationship 'dealbreakers', often end up living through a series of shorter and shorter relationships – until at some point, they give up on them altogether.

One of the main behaviours we develop to protect ourselves from our reactions and the emotions that drive them is to become controlling. This is often most obvious in the shadow stage. We see what we consider inappropriate behaviour and we try and control our partner. However, this exacerbates the problem; even if they do act as we wish them to, they start to resent us and plan their counter offensive or escape.

✓ Try this:

Control and fights go hand in hand and so it is essential in a meaningful and evolving relationship to give up control the best you can. People who are very controlling usually don't have a loving and meaningful relationship, certainly not for any length of time. People who are relaxed and truly accepting manage much better.

Where on this scale do you fit? What do you want to control about your present or past relationships? Do you recognise you have a choice between controlling and cleaning up your past?

Power Struggle Stage Trap 2. Dependence and Independence

Not every relationship hits the shadow trap early on. Sometimes we go from honeymoon directly to the greatest of all lessons in any relationship: the dance of dependence and independence.

As the things that turned us on to our partner suddenly become the very things that turn us right off, we cannot help but feel deeply disappointed, betrayed even. After all, this was the person we had been led to believe would love and cherish us for evermore. Instead, they seem to be oblivious to our needs. So we then fall into the trap of fighting to get our needs met; of insisting our partner change their behaviour in order to make us happy.

✓ Try this:

This scenario typically translates as one partner, say in this case the woman, sulking because of her man's outrageous 'insensitivity'. Meanwhile, he has no idea why she is in such a bad mood. 'What's wrong?' he might ask. 'Nothing!' she replies curtly, folding her arms in front of her. It is a classic case of being angry that her partner doesn't already, telepathically, just *know* what her needs are. We don't realise that, often, we have to teach people how to treat us. If the sulking wife could accept that her husband may not always know what she needs, then she could simply ask him, calmly and clearly, to do what she wants. *'Do I have to spell it out to you?'* she might ask sarcastically. Well, yes, actually, sometimes we do have to spell it out for our partner, whether we are the man or the woman.

The hurt we often feel at our partner's ignorance of our needs, all relates back to our original heartbreak. Unless you grew up in a totally bonded family, then you have needs that weren't met. Those needs then get covered over by our compensations, while the hidden, unacceptable part of us gets transferred onto our most intimate relationships. Having bought into the 'my partner will save me from my pain' myth, our warped logic then makes him or her fully responsible for meeting those needs in us; and that is when the blaming and shaming starts. Yet, as an adult, the only person responsible for our needs, is us.

This fight then results in one partner taking the emotionally dependent position in the relationship.

Even if both of you have been independent people in many areas of your lives, it is not possible to have two independent people in one relationship. This is because all relationships balance.

You both want intimacy, but you find yourself see-sawing between wanting your partner to meet your needs and pretending you don't need anything from them. As one of you takes one position, your partner will naturally move to the opposite position and the relationship starts to polarise. If you are the dependent one, you concentrate on taking care of the needs of your now independent partner. Whilst you as the dependent one are focused on this, your independent partner begins to dissociate, from their own deeper emotions, their own needs and eventually from the relationship itself.

All relationships go through this stage, including non-romantic ones (which is why falling out with a close friend can sometimes feel as heartbreaking as splitting up with a lover). If we don't learn about the dynamics of this step in the power struggle stage we will not 'get' relationships.

OUR STORY: Our Dependent–Independent Dynamic

Sue says:

> I always needed lots of approval, especially from my father when I was growing up. I quickly learned how to be a 'good girl,' did well at school and sports and generally towed the line. Although it wasn't apparent in the early stages of our relationship, once Jeff and I really got together I soon transferred my need for approval onto him by subconsciously replaying the 'good girl' role. This meant I became the capable, sensible

partner who looked after our home, our money and so on and found myself tut-tutting and disapproving of his wilder, less responsible ways.

It was a classic scenario. When we first met I loved Jeff's roving, adventurous spirit. But then the very thing I originally loved about him became a major source of friction and fights, especially when the children came along.

I couldn't figure out why trying so hard to be a good wife and mother was such a turn-off for Jeff. The more I tried, the less attention he paid to me – it was so frustrating. My need for approval extended to needing wider recognition for the trappings of status, so we bought a big old house that needed lots of work and financing. Somehow Jeff's work with boats took him further and further away from home. I was disappointed that he seemed to prefer to be elsewhere, so my need for approval grew. I focused on the house and kids and though things were great when he first came home, the arguments would soon start and then suddenly it was time for another trip.

Although I got lots of approval for what I was doing from friends and family, ('*You're amazing to put up with it!*' and '*What a wonderful job you are doing!*') I craved it from Jeff first and foremost. I tried to get it by testing him to do what I wanted, like washing up or helping in the garden. Then, of course, I would be furious when he failed these 'love tests'. No wonder he felt trapped and as if life was no fun anymore. I was the archetypal dependent partner, practically hanging onto his ankles as he walked out the door, almost begging for his love. I was the emotional, complaining, nagging one and I hated myself for it; it was not the 'me' that I recognised.

Jeff says:

When we hit this stage in our relationship I fought hard to be the independent partner. At that time I thought it was important to be strong and independent, and that meant not becoming emotional. So I did the strong silent number while Sue did the dependent feely number. I fell for all the traps in this stage: the temptations, the belief that things were always greener on the other side of the hill, and would back off once I saw Sue's dependence. I was always looking for the next adventure, not because I really wanted the adventure but because I wanted my independence. If I did stay away for too long I began yearning for home. However, once I got home, these feelings would soon reverse. It took a while, but finally I realised that I was just running away. But when I was home, I expected Sue to take care of my needs, maintain the home and look after the children. It was true that I was bringing home the money but it was certainly not without strings.

This is a complex dynamic that changes over time, but typically the independent partner leads the relationship. They are usually hardworking and charismatic; they insist in needing space, freedom and to have things 'my way or the highway'. They might like to see themselves as a free spirit, whereas, in fact, they are often too scared to commit. Although they are not consciously aware of it, they recoil from commitment because it means all those childhood emotions that were too painful to feel at the time will come up to be dealt with.

It falls to the dependent partner to carry their partner's repressed feelings within the relationship. When things are going well they will feel all the joyful feelings attached to that, but, equally, when things are going wrong – often badly wrong – they get to fully feel those feelings too.

✓ Try this:

Perhaps right now you're feeling that you are more in one camp than the other: the independent or the dependent. Try not to judge yourself, just allow this new realization to settle in.

These questions may help you to pinpoint the dynamics in your present, or a past, relationship. Each description is marked 'i' for independent, or 'd' for dependent.

In your relationship, are you the one who wants to talk about where the relationship is going (d), or the one who finds excuses not to (i)?

Are you the more emotional partner, the one who seems to have all the problems? (d)

Or are you the 'fixer' who comes up with practical, not emotional, solutions? (i)

Do you feel you have become a different person within your partnership, someone you hardly recognise any more? (d) (i)

> Do you think about, worry about or even obsess about your partner more than they think about you? (d)
>
> Or do you wonder what all the fuss is about and wish your partner could get on with their life? (i)
>
> Do you feel your partner is the source of your happiness and security, that your world would fall apart if they left for any reason? (d)
>
> Or are you secretly impatient with all the attention and tempted to look to other people, activities, or perhaps your work, as sources of happiness? (i)
>
> If you recognise any of these dynamics have been in your relationship for some time, then you are polarised in this independent-dependent step.

Emotions take energy. In a particularly polarised relationship, the dependent partner can start feeling burdened by this extra emotional weight on their shoulders. But the dependent partner also has a hidden agenda. To be dependent means you basically think that your partner has something that will make you feel loved, or get attention or feel safe. So the subconscious message of the dependent partner to the independent partner is: *'I will give to you in many ways. I will take care of your needs, but you had better give back to me in this one place of need that I have.'*

It is as if the independent type is dragging themselves around with the dependent one hanging onto their leg. For the dependent, this is hardly a dignified look – for desperation is always a major turn-off. The more of a wet blanket they become, the less attractive they are to their partner. Whilst dependents tend to have all the 'problems' in the relationship, independent types, who are masters of dissociating from their feelings, will have the temptations – to run for the hills, stay out a lot, work far away or fall into the arms of someone else. This is because once the dependent one polarises they become the independent one's worst nightmare. The independent looks at their partner and what they see is what they swore they would never be like again; they swore that never again would they be needy, dependent and emotional – that is the very basis of their independence.

✓ Try this:

If you are the independent partner, your challenge is to have the courage to stay put, move towards and appreciate your partner, be emotionally brave and dare to feel your feelings – and to refrain from judging your 'blubbering wreck' of a partner as weak or over-sensitive. In truth, your dependent partner has been willing to feel all the feelings for both of you, so moving towards your partner emotionally will bring things back into balance.

If you are the dependent partner, your challenge is to let go of your hidden taking agenda and learn to take care of your own needs. Stop manipulating (there are so many forms of emotional blackmail, from sweet-talking or eyelash-batting at one extreme to threats of misery and worse at the other) to get what you want, and stop putting the onus on your partner to fill the emotional 'black hole' inside of you. In truth, your independent partner is doing you a favour because learning to be up front about your needs and not expecting others to take care of them is a huge leap in emotional maturity.

We have worked with many couples who have become totally polarised in this dependent-independent dynamic. It is the reason that most relationships end, just as ours did, because it seems impossible to find the bridge back to each other.

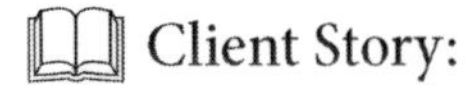

Client Story:

Alan couldn't understand why his wife was so emotional. It drove him crazy when she would 'lose it' and scream at him in public or at family gatherings. He felt he needed a quiet life so he could focus on providing for the family including two demanding teenagers, instead of this emotional roller coaster. It seemed when he tried reasonably and rationally to explain his position he wasn't listened to. Meanwhile Linda hated his 'lectures' and the way he tried to control mealtimes, holidays and everything to do with how he thought things should be. Much as she tried to discuss and keep her cool, she felt the only way she could be heard over his controlled rant was to become over-emotional, and of course the public show was part of her weaponry.

Both Alan and Linda were horrified by their behaviours, by the effect on their family life, and by the personalities they felt they had turned into. When they understood how they had become polarized in their behaviour, they saw that underneath they both felt the same: they both felt unheard, both convinced that their need for respect was disregarded by their partner.

Once they understood their similarities and learned to give up their control, and started to communicate more truthfully and honestly about how they felt, they began to get past the fights.

At the core of any fight are two people struggling to be right about something and the more one partner believes they are right, the other partner will always balance them out and become just as right in the opposite direction. The only way through this dynamic is to stop being right.

We often say that you have to value your relationship and make it more important than your past – and more important than your need to be right.

Power Struggle Stage Trap 3: Polarisation

The next step we learn to navigate in this power struggle stage is what we call the positive-negative dynamic. We can look at this by imagining one partner is a 'Tigger' and the other an 'Eeyore', to use the characters from the famous children's stories of Winnie the Pooh.

Tiggers, the super-positive, annoyingly bouncy ones, have boundless energy, set exciting goals but consistently underestimate the resources it takes to achieve them. To be around a positive like Tigger often means we have to be in sacrifice to their grand goals. They tend to plan things without thinking through the downsides and go charging ahead without seeing any problems or potential pitfalls ahead.

It comes down to the 'gloomy' or negative Eeyore to voice these concerns. But, to Tiggers, this comes across as complaining so they continue to forge ahead regardless. This is why when things go wrong, the words most uttered by an Eeyore are: 'I told you so!' And it is true because Eeyores have a radar for problems, being able to foresee them months ahead, but are at a loss as to how to solve them.

Try this:

If you are Tigger, the positive partner, recognise your partner's ability to flag problems. If you are willing to listen you soon realise that working with your partner, rather than independently, can solve problems more easily and effectively.

If you recognise you have become an Eeyore, the negative partner, then it is about winning back your centre. Speak with your partner about how you are feeling and no matter how they respond, do all you can to return yourself to your centre, let go of the dynamic and be willing to move out of the fight and take the next step in your life.

If this dynamic spirals out of control, it can have disastrous consequences for joint projects and even the future of the relationship. If your relationship is this out of balance, it's important to find a bridge between the two poles by recognising the qualities of each party. Seeking the balance point, you discover the potential for an enormously successful, progressive partnership – and the added bonus of another honeymoon phase.

We have seen this dynamic with many clients and most especially in business, where it is common to emphasise the positive or even demand that employees maintain an upbeat, positive attitude. But the world seeks balance. If an organisation only focuses on the positive, then the negative has to find a way to express itself, which often comes out as complaining or bitching. Colleagues will find time and places to get together to have a moan, say around the water cooler or photocopier.

Jeff says:

In our relationship, I have often been the positive one, hatching wild plans about how to make our fortune. When things didn't work out, Sue has often had to resort to those famous words of the negative one: 'I told you so!' I would then attack her for not supporting me, but I was blind to this positive-negative dynamic.

Recently I was part of a project group and after several meetings I realised I had become the negative one. I would get off the conference call and find myself complaining to anyone who would listen, or even people who would not, about how the team was going the wrong way, how they would never achieve their goals and how I wanted to leave. After a lifetime of being the positive one I now knew how it felt to be the negative. I also knew how to give up being so polarised and move to a more centred position. Once I did so, everyone else involved in the dynamic also made that correction. Once you learn how to work together there is no need for such polarisation.

✓ Try this:

Becoming aware of our tendency to polarize is a brilliant first step to greatly improving our relationships; seeing our partner as our equal is a further good step. We also need to recognise there is only one thing worse than having a really negative complaining partner, and that is **we** become that partner. So appreciation is another key; be thankful that they are willing to take that opposite position and still live with you.

If you wanted to go even further you could spend a whole day and swap positions with your partner and see how that feels. Don't be surprised if your partner does not want to swap back.

Power Struggle Stage - The Six Dynamics of Fighting

All couples fight. It's just that some seem to fight fairer than others. But in truth a fight is a fight and there is no good side or wrong side. No matter how justified we feel, fighting is never a solution. In the beginning however, in the power struggle stage and the push-me pull-me dependent-independent dance, we can easily get stuck in our conflict, absolutely convinced that we are right and the other heinously wrong.

We fight because we are 'on the take,' jostling to get our needs met. At the deepest level every fight is just two people saying: '*You are not taking care of my needs, you are not giving to me in some way.*' As we have seen, the joke is the other doesn't even have what it is we are desperate to get from them. They are mirroring our lost part, not withholding it from us. That gift is right inside us. It is just that finding it can be tricky; it is, invariably, an emotionally painful process. This is why it appears that the one you love the most is the one who hurts you the most. When the pain comes up during an argument with our partner, it can feel so overwhelming that we just assume it must be their fault – because no-one else makes you feel this way, right?

But hang on a minute, isn't this the person you thought was 'the one,' 'the missing piece' in your life? How come after living on cloud nine through the highs of the honeymoon, you are now chucking crockery at each other? Can it really be *all* their fault? We don't think so. But first, we have to understand what is really going on here. We have to understand the feelings that are being triggered – because, remember, we all act because of how we *feel* underneath. Our actions are not logical or rational, especially in an argument. They are coming from the subconscious iceberg.

Welcome to what we call 'The Six Dynamics of Fighting.'

1. We Are Never Upset for the Reasons We Think We Are

When we are upset with our partner, our automatic response is that it is all about now and all about them. But think about it. Think back to the last time your partner (or someone close to you) upset you. Was that the first time such behaviour upset you? Now, focus on the feeling, feel it in your body and breathe into it – it would be helpful if you can take a few minutes to do this now – and then see what it reminds you of. Who did that to you before? How old were you?

With any level of honesty and self-examination, you will soon see how this issue runs like a thread through your life. No doubt it has occurred time and again in very similar circumstances with other people too.

When we are upset we have unfinished business from the past that needs to be cleaned up and resolved. Our upsets show us where we have not seen a particular situation correctly. It actually shows us where we are *wrong* about something.

Now, we know this is not easy. Mostly, when we are upset, we resist allowing the deeper feelings it brings up to just be there, because they are just too painful – so we storm out of the room, or yell at our partner to shut the f*** up, because it is making us feel so bad. Then we defend against having to feel this pain by taking a position of being right about something (like how horrible our partner is) and – bingo – you have a fight on your hands.

You can't be right and be happy. We often say: If you insist on being right, you will soon be dead right. And if you continue being dead right, you will just end up dead! Isn't that, after all, what happens in armed conflict?

In a power struggle the extent to which one side is convinced they are right, is the extent to which the other one believes their position is the right one too. It is important to remember that these are perspectives, not absolute truths.

Jeff says:

A few years ago I was working on a promotion strategy with other trainers within the UK and we came up with an idea we all thought was great and we could get behind. After only a brief period one of the trainers stopped using the strategy and we were heading for a fight. My initial reaction was to push her back into line and sort her out.

> I recognised I had a particular perspective on the situation from which my logic flowed. I felt undeniably right about my position and certain that others needed to follow my lead. The situation was in danger of becoming very polarized when I decided to try another course of action. I became curious about how she had reached her position. What was her thought process? How did she view the world? In a moment of clarity, it flashed on me why she had taken her position and how she felt.
>
> In that moment, the fight was gone and we could work together again toward a resolution that moved us all forward.

Giving up the need to be right is essential in a long-term partnership, yet many people find this frightening; they believe they will be disempowered or 'walked over.' But the answer never comes from just one side. It comes from including and integrating both sides of the conflict. This is called resolution.

Surrendering your position is not about sacrificing yourself. It is about being willing to accept that we may be wrong about the whole answer, although we may be right about part of it. Refusing to give up being right is dangerous. It keeps us locked in the power struggle and means that both parties will lose out in some way – apart from the divorce lawyers, of course. It is a costly process in more ways than one.

We know people who have lost everything – their relationship, home, career, custody of their children – because they could not let go of their need to be right.

This is the work of hubris most vividly displayed. All of us have watched the wreckage of human relationships wash down the river like flotsam after a great storm all because we, a speck on a sea of infinite possibilities, think we are right. We have made being right more important than our partnerships, than happiness, than love, and we wonder why our lives don't turn out for the best.

✓ Try this:

If you are stuck in this position in your relationship, a question you must answer for yourself is this: Is it worth it?

Do you value sufficiently your relationship, or this person, to do the work of healing, delving into your past, learning emotional intelligence and how to expand yourself?

Or is it worth all the conflict just to be right about something you are most likely not right about anyway? How many couples do you know who get dragged through the most messy divorces, fight about every aspect of their lives just to be right or just to score a point over a partner?

If the answer to the first question is 'yes' and the answer to the second is 'no' then your relationship has a chance.

When we think back to our relationship, a turning point was when we began to surrender our positions.

Jeff says:

When I stopped being right about the fact that Sue was the source of my unhappiness, I no longer felt trapped in the marriage or my generally messed up life (not that I would admit it as messed up to anyone). Taking even the smallest amount of responsibility for the situation was enough to start us, or should I say me, in the right direction.

Even after getting back together we still have our fights. I can remember having a blazing row with Sue in our yard. It was one of those finger pointing yelling spectaculars. Then, for an instant, I found myself, or at least my awareness, about 20 feet up in the air looking down as if I was watching a movie. I immediately realised I was not right at all about everything I was yelling and screaming about. I came straight back into my body and immediately apologized to Sue. Later we even had a little laugh about the ridiculousness of the situation.

Sue says:

Once I stopped being right about how wronged I was, my 'victim' persona collapsed and I could see the extent of the distance I had created between Jeff and me. The gulf stretched out behind me like a highway in the desert. In being right about how capable and responsible I was, I might have won the battle for being the 'good one' in some people's eyes, but I had lost my relationship, I had become unreachable and certainly driven the fun out of our life together.

Often people ask us: '*What is the one thing I can do to speed up my growth and give me happiness?*' Our answer is simple. Accept you are not right about anything that you think you are right about. In fact, the more you know, the more you realise how little you can ever possibly know. We are all but tiny specks within the great cosmic mystery of life. To think we can 'know it all' is absurd.

2. Our Perceptions are Projections

According to Carl Jung: '*Just as we tend to assume that the world is as we see it, we naively suppose that people are as we imagine them to be. All the contents of our unconscious are constantly being projected onto our surroundings.*' Freud's perspective was that projection is about seeing our own faults and 'unacceptable desires' in others. His daughter, Anna Freud, called this 'displacement outward.'

Many schools of psychotherapy agree that projection happens; it is just a question of to what degree. The PoV (Psychology of Vision) model we use is radical in that it states that, as our inner and outer worlds are completely interconnected, then our outer world consists entirely of our projections, good and bad.

In our blame and compensation culture this is a challenging idea. But when it comes to intimate relationships, as we have said before, no-one can do anything to hurt you that you are not already, at some subconscious level, doing to yourself.

For example, your partner might, in a fit of rage, call you 'stupid'. If, for example, you had a bullying teacher at school who routinely humiliated you in class, then this would hurt and you would probably retaliate angrily.

The bullying teacher is long gone, but the hurt, which is now your responsibility to resolve and heal, still remains. If, however, inside yourself you know you are kind and intelligent, then the statement would slide by like water off a duck's back. You wouldn't respond emotionally because you wouldn't believe it any more than if your partner told you your ears were green.

OUR STORY: How We Fought Each Other

Sue says:

My biggest problem with Jeff was that I judged him to be totally irresponsible and inconsiderate. I was tortured by wanting him to stick around, do the washing up, read to the kids, live to some kind of recognisable plan – anything to prove he was the responsible husband and father I thought he should be. We would blow up at each other over the silliest little things, like a pile of dirty dishes or mud stains on the carpet. After all the shouting, door-slamming and then listening to his car screech out of the driveway, I would slump back onto the sofa and burst into tears. Here I was left alone with the kids, yet again, my marriage in tatters. I have also been known to chuck wine over him and once punched him on the chin. I laugh about it now, but at the time I was totally miserable.

It was after a PoV workshop on projection when I finally got what our fights were all about for me; it was where I was refusing to accept my irresponsible side. In order to please my father (and therefore be loved) I had repressed the spontaneous, funny, more carefree part of me and judged it as reckless and irresponsible. Once I woke up to this other part of me, I felt so much freer. Before it was like a tug of war with Jeff, neither of us able to meet the other halfway. Neither of us was right or wrong, we were just deluded. What I thought was making me so miserable turned out to be the most wonderful gift – spontaneity.

Jeff says:

Sue was, so I thought, so pedantic and obsessed with details that it drove me crazy. I just couldn't handle being forced to plan things and take responsibilities. Despite my love for her, I felt trapped, like a caged animal, and would react angrily. Even the simplest request to help around the house would trigger a bad reaction and the tension in our house was tangible. I was an unexploded ordinance waiting for the smallest perceived slight.

We did have happy times, enjoying our home with our first born, a great circle of friends, parties, travel, pleasure in each other's company. We also worked together on common goals like our home and the businesses that Sue ran from there.

But as I moved around living this dashing but irresponsible life, the periods of happiness were shorter and then became increasingly rare. In order to cope, I became more distant. I took longer assignments overseas and soon after getting home would be scanning the horizon for the next offer, the next adventure. When I was away I would call home often and have long conversations, well long for me, and we wrote love letters, but when I was home those feelings soon evaporated.

I am so glad I finally came to my senses, for to continue would have been a very destructive path. I was taking greater risks in my life, drinking and smoking heavily. Increasingly distant from my kids, with little thought about their welfare, a divorce would have brought about an abrupt end to that relationship. The future would not have been a new life with a job and another house or wife, but either jail or an early death and certainly no one around to mourn me.

The penny finally dropped when I was sitting on a dock in the Persian Gulf. I knew I was at a crossroads. In one direction lay the wide-open spaces, the endless sea and in the other lay my family. I had always chosen the former, but this time, in a flash of clarity, I realised that the latter was the more difficult choice, the one that would take far more courage and would take me into unknown territory. Yet it had the greatest pull on me now because deep in my heart I really missed my family.

Once I understood my role in the dynamic between Sue and me, an emotional dam burst inside and realisations flooded in. I recognised how overwhelming it would have been for me to assume responsibility in my family of origin, given what was going on. My strategy was to head in the opposite direction.

Growing up as a white farming kid in black Africa with its splits and fractures seemed to mirror my family. The Mau Mau war, an uprising in Kenya between 1952 and 1960, seemed to reflect my relationship with my brothers, which was one long brawl. My mother suffered a series of breakdowns throughout my childhood, most of which, from the age of five, was spent far away from her in a sadistic boarding school. There was a chaotic sense of dysfunction within my family that I wanted no part of.

It took me ten years to recognise that Sue was mirroring back the lost part of me. What I had not bargained for was having to face the pain of why I lost my 'responsible' self in the first place. But by this time there was no going back. Finally understanding the whole conflict meant I was eventually able to deal with it quickly and easily. The result was worth every step.

3. Inner Splits Cause Outer Splits

Whenever we are in conflict, our partner is mirroring back to us a place where we are conflicted in our minds. We have identified with one side of the conflict and buried the other, which our dearly beloved dutifully acts out on our behalf.

Remember the society lady who hated bad manners, yet always attracted men who acted this out? Like her, we identify with one side (good manners) and blame, judge and banish the other side (bad manners). Our higher mind seems to have a habit of attracting these very people into our lives in order to bring the issue to light – and to therefore be healed.

✓ Try this:

In the best-case scenario you would see your partner's angry outburst as a cry for help. You would see that they were hurting, but wouldn't take it personally. Being able to stand in a neutral, non-judging – indeed compassionate – place is the best way to dissolve an argument. So, when you find yourself getting stuck in bad feeling towards your partner for their appalling behaviour towards you, you might like to remind yourself that you have something to learn here. You might even want to mentally thank them for bringing this issue up for you to finally resolve and move on from. When you release your judgments of others, you release your own judgments of yourself – and buried self-judgment (self-criticism) always holds us back in life.

4. Underneath a Fight, Each Person is Feeling the Same

When we are locked in a power struggle, we see the other as our adversary, the cause of all our bad feelings. But what we are really fighting for is to avoid feeling our own original overwhelming pain. Whenever we work with couples in conflict, it always turns out that their deepest, most painful emotions driving the whole dynamic, are actually the same.

Let's say the deepest, most painful emotion in each partner is a fear of abandonment. Remember that was part of the original attraction; both people have the same issue! The dependent partner will be the one holding and feeling this fear within the relationship. They will act fearfully and hang onto their partner with all their might, in a desperate attempt to never feel abandoned again. The independent one will have fully dissociated from their fear of abandonment, having promised themselves to *never be in the position* to be abandoned again. They will, therefore, usually jump ship first (just as their dependent partner feared) in order to stay safely dissociated from their core pain. So one partner will stay home and feel the issue, in this case abandonment, and the other will act on the feeling by doing the abandoning. Each partner acts in opposite ways, yet each partner has the same deep, unresolved issue.

You may have seen this dynamic with friends who talk to you individually about what is going wrong in their relationship. When you get to speak to them they complain about what the other is doing and these complaints are often the same. She does not listen to me; he does not listen to me! Certainly they may be acting differently but actually they are feeling the same.

✓ Try this:

Take a few moments and look at what you are blaming your partner for and then take a further moment and honestly look at when you are doing the same, maybe not exactly the same actions but with the same resulting feelings. Honesty is the best policy!

What's interesting about complaining and blaming is that if you have the courage to look at your behaviour with any clarity you will soon realise you are culpable of what you point the finger at in others. We typically hide our own behaviour under the guise of being right about their's. We love to play good guy - bad guy.

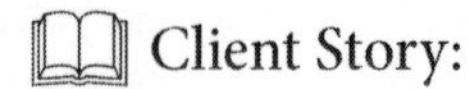

One couple we worked with both had deep insecurities from being bullied at school as young children. The independent partner, in this case the man, was a bully around the house and would lash out in fury. His wife, the dependent partner, became like a timid mouse at home, even though she was a much-loved teacher in her career. Their behaviour was opposite but both partners had the same feelings of inadequacy deep down. Once we focused on the similar underlying feelings their behaviour toward each other changed. Understanding that they shared the same deeper emotions brought their issues to light, allowing them to feel more of a team. Why would they attack each other when they saw they were the same? They glimpsed the light of reconciliation at the end of the tunnel.

5. The Dilemma: Should I Stay or Should I Go?

One of the most important things to learn about getting past our fights is that it requires courage, communication and trust, because we need to work together to resolve our issues. If we are in a fight with our partner and we believe leaving the relationship will solve the problem, we are making a big, big mistake. Just because we might have left our partner, doesn't mean we have left the issue. It will follow us into our next relationship and, again, we will come to the same point. Often people quit their relationship because it 'doesn't work.' But they then find the same issue with their friends, or, even worse, with their kids.

Because we have been taught that fighting is generally a 'bad thing', some of us find it extremely uncomfortable. We see it as bad behaviour and don't want to be a part of it. The tendency then is to withdraw. We adjust to the conflict, start pitying our angry, petty, nasty, sometimes violent partner, rather than deal with the issues head on. This kind of compromise only serves to enable and prolong the conflict. In fact, you might be surprised to know that there is as much aggression in withdrawal as there is in attack.

When we withdraw we pull away from our partner, we shut down and become totally unavailable to our partner and totally unavailable to a resolution. This is an act of aggression and certainly feeds the fight energy in a relationship.

Sometimes we stay in conflict in order to avoid moving forward in life. In truth, any form of power struggle is a form of delay. We have become frightened of learning, growing and taking the next step in our lives – the next issue our subconscious has thrown up in order to be healed. Typically we will stay in this conflict until we have the courage to surrender to our own deeper feelings and reclaim the missing piece of ourselves. Once we have done so, the next step becomes clear – we don't have to look for it or agonise about what the next step is, whether we should stay or go. The resolution reveals itself to us when we have cleared our inner debris out of the way.

This is a scary place because it requires a deep trust in life and in yourself to bring this all to a good conclusion. It also requires trust and confidence in our partner, something that will have most likely been eroded throughout the power struggle.

✓ Try this:

Choose to see your partner as your ally, not your enemy. We appreciate that a violent or abusive partner needs more intervention than we are discussing here; we are assuming that there is a willingness to learn and a level of emotional maturity where physical violence is not an issue.

Even though the methodology might vary in interventions of abuse and violence, the principles remain the same. We do ask that the readers (assuming more than one) suspend two beliefs the best they can: the first is that there are good guys and bad guys in a relationship and the second is that it takes two to tango. This second belief is really just the first step in creating the first and neither is helpful or constructive in sorting out relationship problems because you need to give your trust towards the best possible outcome rather than the worst one. Every good coach or teacher knows this. They see the potential, whilst acknowledging the problem. They work for the highest outcome and focus on the best. Conflicts are inevitable but withdrawal is not the solution. It is feeling our feelings and giving of ourselves that ends conflicts.

Don't miss the opportunity to resolve your fight with your partner, so you can really move on with your life – whether that turns out to be with them or without them.

6. All Relationships Balance

It is easy to view our partner as the bad or difficult one, the one causing all our relationship problems; or to see our friends' relationships as unevenly balanced into a 'good guy, bad guy' scenario. In our work we see all relationships, no matter how polarised, as perfectly balanced. The extent to which one of us is out of balance the other is out of balance in some other way to the same extent.

To have a successful and happy relationship it is important to develop a no-blame, no-fault policy and instead make it about learning the dynamics of what is really going on between two people in a close relationship. It is important to learn to recognise when you are beginning to polarise and while it is natural to some extent; when we become too polarised we deepen the power struggle which ultimately is costly for both parties.

You might want to take a breath while you let this perspective sink in. It can take a big mental leap to accept total responsibility for your feelings within a difficult relationship, especially if you are prone to 'stamp-collecting'; making 'what you have done wrong to me' lists in your head. The bottom-line is that no-one can do anything to hurt you that you are not already doing to yourself in some way, albeit on a deeper subconscious level. The reason we know this is because we lived it out, somewhat dramatically, in our own relationship.

OUR STORY: It Only Takes One to Change the Relationship Dynamic

Sue says:

By 1989, our relationship had deteriorated into an 'ask your father to pass the salt' situation and so we separated for two years. When I finally served divorce papers on Jeff, I was left in terrible emotional turmoil. I would ruminate about him and our problems for hours at a time. What might he have said or done if I had done this or that instead? Was I really so unattractive? How could I get him to stay in touch with the kids even if he didn't want to see me?

Then a friend lent me a Chuck Spezzano tape where he talks about his spiritual journey and how he developed the PoV model. The tape helped me realise that there was absolutely nothing I could do to change Jeff and make him into the father and husband I thought he should be. I just got it: the only person I could change was myself, and the pattern I had that had led me to being such an emotional, dependent partner.

I accepted everything about Jeff and energetically let him go. I felt so free and light, it was wonderful. Then, within a matter of days, he showed up at the door! I was astounded; it was the last thing I was expecting or even wanting at this point. I thought I was sorted and didn't need him anymore. I had even started another relationship.

Now Jeff was offering to be the proper father and husband I had been wishing for so desperately and was begging me to take him back. But I couldn't be sure he would be any different so I said no. Then he picked up a PoV workshop brochure that a friend had left at the house. That was a big turning point for both of us. He came back from the first workshop a different man, his energy was less pushy and insistent, he was more available and willing to talk. Suddenly it wasn't all my fault anymore and we talked without blame about what had gone wrong. He kept doing workshops and after each one would tell me what he had learned about himself. I started to think that we might have a chance to make it as a couple, though I held out for a few months before I admitted I was ready to trust the change.

Jeff says:

When Sue served divorce papers on me I remember driving away in horrendous emotional pain. But I had no idea what to do about it, apart from drink, have more affairs and take jobs further and further away from it all.

As I have said, I was captaining a tug boat 4,000 miles away in the Persian Gulf when I woke up one morning and knew I had changed. It never ceases to amaze me that this was about the time that Sue energetically let go of me completely.

At the time I had no idea why, but I simply couldn't play the macho captain and give orders any more. My psychological façade was crumbling; I was awash with emotions – the pain was coming in waves – and desperate to get back to Sue.

Leaving that ship was a big deal. There was a lot at stake financially and my superior was a very hard macho type. I thought: *'If I get out of here with most of my limbs intact I'm a lucky man.'* I was quaking in my boots when I told him I was resigning for the sake of my family and my marriage. He then looked me straight in the eye and said he wished that he had had the courage to make that decision.

I flew home the next day an emotional wreck and begged Sue to take me back. Thank goodness she said no. It meant I had to do things I swore I never would, like therapy, which meant really facing up to myself. I went from one extreme to the other by experimenting with yoga and meditation, mainly to impress Sue.

Then I tried a PoV workshop with Chuck and Lency Spezzano and I was hooked. Time and again in workshops, I would watch Chuck unveil the subconscious dynamics beneath people's relationship problems.

He helped me see where my need to rebel and have affairs came from. The strict, humiliating regime at boarding school caused me to shut down emotionally to survive. This fuelled my compulsion to rebel and live an 'adventurous' life. Also, my father quite openly had affairs. I learned that when we judge our parents' actions as bad, we will then either grow up and do the same thing, as I did, or we swear we will never be like that. But often we will treat ourselves as if we had acted in that way, or our partner will act it out.

These were the first of many lessons I needed to learn but it was such a relief to understand why I was acting the way I was. My life started to make sense. For the first time, I felt I was the captain of my life. I was able to start steering my own ship, rather than be unwittingly steered by my subconscious pain.

Our relationships are a source of great learning and an ever-unfolding dance that will take us to the doors of bliss if we keep a good attitude about our learning. But when we become right and stuck in a fight we have stopped learning and when we stop learning in a relationship it starts dying.

Chapter 6

THE DEAD ZONE STAGE

'Oh baby, baby, where did our love go?'

The Supremes

There is a saying that opposites attract. If this is the case in your relationship, then you are likely to spend more time in the power struggle stage, working through and getting past the differences. Other couples who are more similar to each other end up spending more time in the dead zone, the next and final stage to be navigated on the way to partnership.

In the honeymoon stage we give everything we have to our new partner. We give our fun, our spontaneity, our sexuality and all this giving makes it a honeymoon. However, at some point we find we have no more great gifts to give. Instead, we have only the broken bits of our lives, the things we feel guilty about, our weaknesses, our failures, our strange bathroom habits and the things we did to small furry animals when we were children.

This isn't what we want to show our partner. We fear they might leave us if we told them about all our human failings, if we scare them by rattling all the skeletons in our cupboards. So we hide our broken pieces and start acting out what we think we should be; an attentive husband, a loving supportive wife, a good parent. But these are not you; it is like you have made a cardboard cutout of yourself, someone who runs on autopilot, who has lost all spontaneity. The real you has stepped back.

You now live out a recipe, you now live out a role, you do the right thing but for the wrong reasons. This inauthenticity creates distance between you and your partner – and the loss of contact then creates deadness. We are so busy being who we *should* be, rather than who we actually are, it feels like all the fun, the passion, the enthusiasm, the sex and the sense of living a full life has been sucked out of you. Thus we enter the biggest trap in our lives, the place that relationships die in, marriages die in and we die in. We reach (cue foreboding music: dum dum duuuum) the dead zone.

Life in the Dead Zone

If you have reached the dead zone in your relationship, you have reached a place of some success. You have been together for a while. Mostly you are past the stage of telling your partner you are going to leave them every time something goes wrong. Maybe you have reached middle to top management level in your career or you own your own company or practice. Even if you have achieved a modicum of financial security or success, with some material trappings of stability, the partner, the kids, the house, the car, the dog, the cat – the key is that you can't feel it.

We have reached a plateau, yet we feel more of a failure than before. At the very least, we expect feelings of worthiness, happiness and wellbeing to be the pay off for working so hard to 'be someone'. But unless happiness and self-worth are there at the beginning, no amount of worldly success will provide it. Many capable, skilled, clever, successful people are secretly terrified of being found out for the 'fraud' that deep down they believe they are. Typical sayings of people who are trapped in the dead zone reflect this refusal to admit any failure: *'when the going gets tough the tough get going,'* or *'I have to carry everyone'*, or their view of leadership could be summed up as 'it's lonely at the top!' As these subtle feelings of deep failure take hold, we try several ways to keep this deadness at bay; we might make ourselves too busy to have to think about it by overworking, or become lazy, depressed or indulgent (alcohol, recreational drugs, food, shopping, shoes and so on). Left unaddressed the dead zone can lead to burn out – and the trap of working hard and then playing hard to compensate.

In the dead zone, sex is some form of duty and no longer a spontaneous, exciting encounter. In the dead zone we often need more and more stimulation to experience the briefest of feelings. We look for something exciting to do just to get some adrenalin going again. We become kinkier, take up extreme sports or buy a growling Harley Davidson motorbike – anything to inject some intensity back into our lives.

Some of us come home and provoke our partner. We yank their chain just to get a reaction because we can't stand the deadness. Finally at some point, often around the age of 40, the deadness becomes too much and we hear that voice inside our head that says: *'Run! Get the hell out.'* So we give up our job, we give up our family and we head for Australia to open a bar on Bondi Beach in the belief it will give us our life back. Sure, it will be great for a while, in the honeymoon stage, but as the old saying goes: *'Wherever you go, there you are.'* It is only a matter of time before the old pattern repeats and the deadness creeps back. The problem is not out there. It is inside us.

Men are especially susceptible to a dead zone related mid life crisis, and the point of explaining it here is to show you what drives people to look outside their relationship for excitement. This is the time when couples are most susceptible to having affairs, when people are desperate to get some of those honeymoon feelings back.

Women's and men's lifestyle magazines are forever printing articles on 'how to get the spark back' into your relationship and your sex life. Yes, you can try everything from bondage to romantic getaways, but unless the underlying causes are dealt with, this is merely a distraction - fun for a while but not a long-term solution. In the dead zone we have lost the ability to feel and without feeling everything, everyone becomes just an object.

OUR STORY: When Our Spark Went Out

Jeff says:

When I was in the dead zone with Sue I was no longer attracted to her physically. At one time I saw everyone outside of our relationship as desirable but not her. I would have sworn on a stack of bibles that the spark had gone, never to return. Once I had got through my transformation and come out of the dead zone, all the passion and fun and physical contact came back and has continued over the years.

I often read articles about how to put the life back into marriages, sometimes even by suggesting it is OK to have affairs. Thing is, I know that when you do that, you close the door on true happiness. You confuse success with adrenalin and you lock yourself even deeper into the dead zone.

Sue says:

When we stopped fighting outwardly, we just sank into this dreadful sameness. Every day, every conversation, every time we made love... it all seemed so predictable. There seemed no way out of it without fighting, so I just gave up. I retreated into my cardboard cutout of the resigned, mildly depressed but capable person, keeping it all together. Underneath I felt like a failure but I couldn't admit it, so I covered it up and soldiered on. It took our break up to shake me out of the dead zone.

Many people have said to us that they get on better with their ex-partner now they are no longer together, and this is because they feel they can be themselves again without the mysterious dynamics of power struggle and dead zone seeming to run their lives. When Jeff and I split up we finally started talking more honestly than ever before, and once we understood why we had got into such an unhappy state we have moved on to find more authenticity, freedom and genuine excitement in each other.

Traps in the Dead Zone

The dead zone is a tricky place, littered with traps, snares and pitfalls. When we get stuck here it is easy to give up on the relationship, to believe that love has died. However, this is not the time to give up, avoid or run away. It is, in fact, the time to commit to getting through this desolate place together, because it is here where our learning is; it is here where we are being shown what inner blocks are holding us back, not just in love but in life itself. So, let's take a look at the four major traps most people stumble upon in this place.

These are: first - roles, rules, duties and being in 'fusion' with our partner (rather than being healthily bonded). The second - staying stuck in our original childhood family dynamics. Third - we have been competing with our partner or others around us; and lastly - there is our fear of change, of taking the next step and moving forward in life.

Dead Zone Stage Trap 1: Roles, Rules, Duties & Fusion

ROLES

A **role** is a persona we have created in response to a situation. We are doing the right things but for the wrong reasons. Most of us have a number of roles and each one is like a suit of armour with the real us hidden inside. Our roles were formed when we were young and something went wrong in our lives, or with our families. On some level this has happened to every one of us, and when it did we made a number of choices about how life is, how men are, how women are, and so on. All those choices create belief systems, which we then bury in our subconscious mind. It is these hidden deep-set beliefs that, as the saying goes, 'create our reality.'

✓ Try this:

Let's imagine that, as a child, you were told off for doing something 'stupid' and, feeling humiliated, you believed that this was actually true. From this situation, one of the internal choices you would most likely have made would be: 'From now on

I have to be clever.' The 'have to' message will then create a role of being very clever, which of course is not necessarily a bad thing – except that this role has been created on the bones of a childhood trauma. It is built to compensate for the hidden belief you really are stupid. Later in life, you will typically react badly to people who you perceive as being stupid, especially if it is your beloved partner. And, of course, you will be super-sensitive to criticism or any perceived inference that you are 'stupid.'

Thinking you are stupid or clever may not be your exact issue, but what gives these compensations away is your strong emotional reaction. What issue triggers that strong emotional reaction for you?

Our strong emotional reaction is what gives a role or the underlying belief away. When we cannot stand to be around people we 'see' this way, or when someone accuses us of being 'stupid'. During our seminars each participant is paired up with a buddy and one of the purposes of this is to find the negative beliefs we have buried in our sub-conscious mind. There seems to be an unseen force that draws people who trigger our hidden aspects, towards us. We don't believe that this happens for life to punish us in some way; we believe that there is a part of us that wants us to heal, that wants us to deal with these negative beliefs about ourselves.

The truth in these situations is not that you are your roles, nor is it true that you are 'stupid'. Most likely the reason that you were called stupid is because the person or parent that told you off for being stupid was feeling that they were stupid, and they were feeling stupid because of something that had happened to them when they were kids and most likely they had hidden that with a role. This is how traumas pass from generation to generation and the only question for us is, when is it going to stop?

During the course of our lives we create a number of roles; roles of being a good person, a hard worker, a good parent.

You know you are in role because, sooner or later, you feel like you are stuck in a rut, which leads to exhaustion. It feels like no matter how hard you try, it is never good enough; the rewards, the approval you hope to gain, never come your way. All the reward goes to the role, which is not the authentic you.

There comes a time for many of us when our role collapses, usually through the sheer exhaustion of 'carrying' this 'armour.' It usually gets worse before it gets better as the buried feelings of failure and depression are finally let loose. Our first instinct is often to try and embrace the role again but that actually doesn't help, as these bad feelings are not about the present moment but about when we chose our role as a small child.

When we have a collapsing role, the deepest part of our feeling is the desire to give up, to just lie down and die. It is important to recognise these feelings and also realise we do not need to act on them. In fact, all that is needed is to simply be aware and stay with the feelings – although, of course, this takes time and is not necessarily easy. Quite the opposite. However, if we just stay with the feeling and keep choosing life, no matter how shaky we might feel inside, at some point the whole role will drop away, like a dead leaf falling from a tree. Yes, a part of you is dying. But it is not 'you' that will die, only an inauthentic part of your skewed ego structure. When it disintegrates, the gap it leaves makes room for your true, authentic self to emerge.

When we start to become our true selves we no longer try to hide. We are willing to be authentic about what we feel and what we think, not in an aggressive or preachy way but simply because that is who we are: sometimes great and sometimes not so great but always real. We know when we have let go of a role because we experience more of the good things; we have more passion, life is more exciting and the old feelings of burnout and exhaustion have fallen away. We start feeling good about what we do and can let in the reward and acknowledgement for our achievements, which then fuels us to greater heights of intimacy in our relationship and success in our careers.

Client Story:

Many years ago an elegant and wealthy woman stood up in a workshop. She owned a string of spas and wellness centres. On the surface she had it all, but when I asked her if she was happy the answer was no. She was caught in a role, and her role was that of the hard worker. This persona started when she was a young child and her father had attacked her for being lazy. She had repressed the incident, but she had created the role to earn her father's approval. Throughout school and later in her career this drive led to achieving great wealth and material success, but underneath all the apparent success was buried an old childhood trauma that was rooted in her failure to make her father happy. This failure is what her success was built on and as she spoke about it she hinted she had this underlying feeling of wanting to give up.

I have worked with enough people to know that on the surface a feeling of wanting to give up is really the tip of an iceberg; underlying that is a place where we just want to give up in the most serious and final way. When I asked how much time she spent thinking about committing suicide, even I was shocked by her reply. She said she spent about eight hours a day thinking about it, and the only thing that stopped her was the thought of how it would hurt her son.

We took her back to the original incident and let her explore what was going on for her father and his reasons for responding the way he did and how he felt about his behaviour. She forgave him and herself and was able to heal this fracture in her mind. She could then give up the 'had to' internal message and instead could make a choice to work hard. Making a choice from our free will instead of from the role makes all the difference. So from then on she could start working hard for the right reasons; she could feel good about her success and start to enjoy her life, sharing that with her son, instead of spending hours a day trying to work out how to end it.

Experiencing the collapse of a role can be a tumultuous time. The gap it creates can leave us disorientated, even facing great death temptation, but it also frees us up to move forward to greater success in both love and life itself. We learn that the persona, the role never was authentically us. Similarly, the devastating feelings of being a fraud or a failure were all just as false, no matter how 'real' it felt at the time. It is vital to be willing to give up our roles; if we build our whole life upon them, sooner or later when the role collapses, it will all coming crashing down around us. Once we have learnt this lesson, we can help our friends and family as we recognise when their roles are collapsing and coach them through this powerful process.

RULES

Most of us enter a relationship with a set of rules, some of which we communicate to our partner but some we don't. In fact, we don't see why we should have to tell them because they are supposed to love us, and if they love us then they will telepathically just know our rules already, right? The trouble is, we may have contradictory rules, which even confuse us at times – and you can bet that at some point your partner will end up breaking your rules. Such 'crimes' become the cause of many a relationship breakup.

There is a rule about rules: they are there to be broken. Needless to say, when that happens, it triggers a lot of emotions. This is because in the past when something went wrong, instead of pulling out the root cause of our pain we buried it and then created a rule in the belief it would protect us from the past hurt.

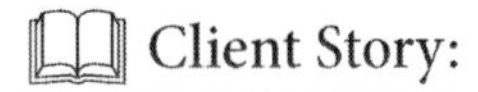

During one of our workshops in Taiwan, a man spoke about how his marriage had broken down. When we asked him why, he told the story of how it was important to him that his wife was always on time. At the beginning of the marriage she had always been very punctual. However, seven years on she had become less and less punctual and they had started to fight about this. She was breaking his rule and they were in huge conflict about it.

We traced the origin of his rule to a childhood incident when his mother had repeatedly called him in from the street for his dinner. He had ignored her and subsequently he got hit by a motorcyclist and landed up in hospital with terrible facial injuries. He had buried all this pain, and while he remembered the incident, he had repressed the emotions. To protect himself from these emotions he had subconsciously created a rule: 'You must never, ever be late!' When his wife broke his rules he over-reacted because the situation was triggering all this childhood pain, pain which he now had the opportunity to heal.

When we create rules to defend our vulnerability, to protect ourselves from feeling that original pain, all we do is put ourselves and those around us into a straightjacket. The more rules, the more boring – and therefore dead – our life becomes.

✓ Try this:

We are not suggesting we should live a life of anarchy. But we do suggest that you could choose to live by principles. Rules you can't dialogue about but with principles you can; and as you grow they can grow with you. An example of a principle would be: 'I would never do anything knowingly to hurt you.' Or: 'I commit to being the best partner I can be.'

DUTIES

These have an aspect of roles and rules; we feel we must carry out our duty to the family, to our friends, or to our country. Of course, it can be a good thing to honour and be loyal to others. But if it comes from a feeling that we 'have to' then it is inauthentic. Our duties become constricting and lead to a level of dissociation that typifies the dead zone. They do not come with passion and enthusiasm but often with growing resentment and deadness. It feels as if our duty – whether that be to society, family or tradition – is telling us that we don't have a choice.

Many times we hear in our seminars and workshops, 'but I have no choice!' And this feels true if we have painted ourselves into such a corner we no longer believe that we do. Or we might respond so habitually that we consciously skip the moment of choice. The first step in correcting this is to increase our awareness about the fact we are making choices and secondly about what those choices are.

Client Story:

One client described a dilemma with her elderly mother, who had reached the stage of needing full time care. Fiona was an artist, and the only one of four siblings without a family of her own. She knew her mother hated the thought of moving to a home, she wanted to look after her mother, but the weight of the duty was overwhelming. Why should she be the one to take this on, why not the others? What about her own life?

We helped Fiona to see how, in the past, she had often made the choice to sacrifice herself out of duty to the family. Once she had forgiven herself and the family, she could ask herself what she really wanted, and she was able make the genuine choice to move in with her mother. It was nearly two years before her mother died, and Fiona told us she was so glad they had shared that time. Her brothers and sister had helped, and everyone was at peace in the family.

Jeff says:

I used to react when I perceived some behaviour in another that I did not particularly like, and within a millisecond I would be angry or moody or upset. I totally skipped the fact that I was choosing my response and often blaming others for my state. The first and most important thing was to start taking responsibility for my state of mind, instead of blaming others. If I was upset then it was because I had chosen to be upset. If I felt I had to do something then it was because I had also made that choice. Even if I started to believe I had no choice that too was a choice.

This is a cornerstone of our teaching: Recognise what you have chosen because it is what is happening. You have chosen it because it is what you feel, you have chosen it because it is your reality. It is essential to recognise this dynamic if you wish to take your power back in your life, because you are choosing now in the present and have been ever since you were a small child. You can always make a new choice as soon as you accept that you are the one who has been making the choices all along. You can make a new choice that is not so unhelpful or self-defeating as one you have made in the past maybe many times, but one that gives you the direction in life that you consciously want.

Now we recognise we can make a new choice we can consciously choose to or choose not to do something and that will make all the difference as the behaviour we choose will not come with a sense of burden. In some areas of our lives we might need to choose more than once, in fact when it comes to relationships, we need to choose thousands of times.

✓ Try this:

Think of a situation in your life now that you feel is a duty. It could be anything, maybe caring for an elderly relative, staying in a job you dislike, cleaning the house, or a relationship you feel trapped in.

When that voice in your mind says, 'I have to . . . . .', doesn't it feel like a burden, a heavy depressing load in your life?

Now substitute 'I have to...' with, 'I choose to...'. Feel the emotional and energetic difference in this new internal message.

And maybe another question arises which is, 'do I **really** choose to?' If so, is there some way this situation can be what you really choose, that is a more successful solution for everyone including you?

As you claim your choice, you claim back your power in your life in relation to this situation.

FUSION

You know you are in fusion with your partner when you moan about your partner to your friends. 'Ah, women!' you might say in an exasperated tone, rolling your eyes. 'Can't live with them, can't live without them.'

If you really cannot live with or without your partner, then you are not healthily bonded. Instead, you are in fusion. It is a dynamic that started (yes, you guessed it) way back in our original family, at a time of trauma or pain when we lost that strong sense of self and of our place in a loving bonded family. It is where we lost our boundaries, where we lost our sense of where we end and others begin. We over-identify with others and take on their emotions as if they were our own. Other times we hide that over-identification and act like we just don't care.

 Client Story:

When Helen's second daughter developed meningitis at the age of six months Helen had to go to hospital with her, where she stayed for several weeks. During that time the baby girl had several fits and no-one knew how good her recovery would be. When Helen came home with her baby, she was exhausted and frightened. She worried that she might lose her little baby and even her elder child, so she held them very close and was scared to leave them. Understandably, she became fused with them.

> As the children grew, the symptoms of this underlying feeling were that every time she left the room, the daughters started fighting. Everyone had become very dependent on each other to the point that every separation caused fear.

This dynamic can show up in a relationship when it seems you start getting too close. The intimacy becomes scary and so fights break out; so you move apart. But when you get too far apart, you start missing them, so you try to find a distance that works. But it is the distance that creates the deadness. When we have fusion running typically we spend a lot of time thinking or talking about 'boundaries,' but in truth it would be far better to learn about bonding and developing a strong sense of self.

You know you are in fusion when:

- Communication is difficult or non-existent. No matter how much you explain your position, your partner never seems to 'get it.' In fact, they respond in a way that shows they haven't heard a word you have said. Most likely you have not been able to hear a word they have said either.

- You can't live with them yet you can't live without them. One minute you love them and are desperate for some affection, the next you can't stand them and want to run away.

- As fusion is a place of lost boundaries and entanglement, not knowing where you end and the other begins, you have to put up defensive 'shields' in order to get a sense of who you are. Often in the relationship you set rules about 'my space.' You may physically create a no-go area or attend seminars about setting up stronger boundaries.

- You return home happy, walk into the house and find your partner in a bad mood. Within minutes you feel miserable too.

- You see your partner as better or worse but not equal to you. Love can only happen between two people who see each other as equals.

- You feel you have 'lost' yourself in the relationship. You then get confused about what you truly want in life.

- You fear true intimacy as you might 'lose yourself'. Yet only people who have already 'lost' themselves ever seem to fear doing so again.

In a bonded relationship you have a full sense of who you are and you can share that with your partner easily. Communication, love and gratitude towards each other just flows.

You know you are bonded when:

- You have strong self-knowledge. You know where you end and other people start. You can be empathic with others but not lose yourself to them.

- You feel a strong connection that transcends time and space. If you are bonded with your children or partner you can feel them wherever they are and sense how they are doing.

- Bonding brings a feeling of equality, an ability to share, and the sense of inclusion. Everyone is an equal member of the family and no one feels alone.

- You can easily communicate ideas and feelings.
- You achieve success with ease, as your mind is no longer split and going in different directions.
- You love easily.

OUR STORY: Being in Fusion

Sue says:

Our relationship had strong elements of fusion before we split up. We found it difficult to communicate what was really going on for us. Neither of us felt the other person could 'hear' us, so we each felt misunderstood and resentful. When we were apart we wanted to be together and our phone calls were full of loving and longing. But when we were together we wondered how soon we could be apart again. Now, we see the patterns of how much we had lost our sense of self in our original families, and our communication is truer and we each feel listened to. But there are still times, particularly in our business dealings, when the old fusion patterns surface. We have learned to be more vigilant for that flashing light of fusion – any area of unclear communication.

✓ Try this:

Take a moment and bring to mind a recent misunderstanding with someone close, an incident which hurt or frustrated you. What happened and who was involved in the recent incident?

> Now as you are in touch with the feeling, trace it back like a thread to what this situation reminds you of from your original family. What happened and who was involved in the original incident?
>
> Can you now imagine that you cut through the bindings of this untrue fusion and forgive everyone in that earlier scene? As you visualize this, feel a greater freedom to be yourself, to be authentic in your present everyday life.

Dead Zone Stage Trap 2: Family Dynamics, Sacrifice & Indulgence

FAMILY DYNAMICS

People often complain to us that their partner is failing them in some way. Often they say things like: *'He has turned out to be just like my father.'* Or: *'She is not the woman I married. She speaks to me just like my mother did!'*

Facing our family dynamics will happen sooner or later in any relationship, because all our relationship patterns come from our family patterns. We turn our partner into our parent, or sibling or other family member and now the issues you had with them, you have to work out with your sweetheart. The only real question is, who are you going to clean up your act with? We all need to clean it up with someone. So, if we don't do it with our original family then we will end up doing it with our partners. And if we decide to leave them, we will either play it out with the next partner or be forced to work it out with our kids. Ah, family! You might be living on the other side of the planet, your parents may even be dead, but there is no escaping those family dynamics.

We have learned that, whatever the experience of our childhood family, it became what we created in our present family. Not only that, whatever we judge our parents for, we will become. *'Oh my God,'* you might say to yourself as you hit your dead zone mid life crisis, *'I have become just like my mother! And I swore I would never be like her.'*

OUR STORY: The Family Dynamics in Our Relationship

Jeff says:

Growing up on a farm in Kenya, submerged into two very different cultures, was never going to be plain sailing. It was exciting and adventurous in many ways, but I now recognise that I judged my father for never being there for me when I was a child. I was packed off to boarding school at the age of five and, even in school holidays, my two brothers seemed to get most of the attention.

When I started to examine myself and to take responsibility for my behaviour, one of the first things I realised was I had done to my son exactly what I had judged my father for. Yes, my son had had some great adventures with me on boats, but for long periods of time I had been absent from his early life. This realisation busted me wide open and motivated me to start to clean up my act. Naturally it was a short step to recognise that I had also been very absent from my marriage.

Sue says:

We never talked about feelings in my childhood family. It was all about who was going where when, why and how. I see that I recreated that same kind of practical communication with Jeff and the children. The underlying feelings were never labelled or acknowledged, it was always about what we were going to do.

Then, when our son went to secondary school he suddenly seemed less communicative; he would come home and go straight to his room. I missed him and it tortured me that he no longer told me about his day. By then I had started understanding that it was up to me to communicate with him, so I began to tell him more honestly and deeply what was going on for me, about all the stuff I was seeing differently. I managed to do it without expecting him to respond in any particular way, and it felt better and more open. Gradually we moved back into balance and he started confiding in me once more.

We are all destined to go further than our original families, to learn from them but to build our own lives. Freeing ourselves from our family dynamics can be a difficult and painful process depending on the circumstances. Some therapists advise leaving the original family behind, but we would say our freedom lies in accepting, forgiving and integrating every judgment or projection. This is not something that can be done overnight. It takes willingness, practise and commitment – just like all relationships in fact.

In some cases, families can be so toxic or so violent it is better that people distance themselves rather than remain in an abusive environment. We fully recognise it is not helpful to remain in such a situation, analysing the dynamics and hoping things will change. However, at some point every situation needs to be revisited, to change the choices and subsequent life patterns we made, so that they do not frame our future.

In our experience it is not the severity of the situation that is important but the choices that we made as a result. Why do some people who grew up in relative ease and plenty, a so-called good family, struggle in their own family later in life? How can others who grew up in desperate and deprived childhoods have loving and successful families in the present? The key factor is our emotional response to what happened, rather than the circumstances themselves.

It may seem irrelevant to revisit our childhood experiences. Many people initially tell us that this is all in the past and there is no point focusing on it now. But remember that these experiences set the patterns for us as adults. When you look back on a distressing childhood incident and make another choice from the perspective of a wiser, older adult, you free yourself from that dynamic and you also free your children from repeating the dynamic. One of the sayings we have is: 'It is never too late to have a happy childhood!'

SACRIFICE & INDULGENCE

Many people believe that they can't have their own life *and* be in a close, meaningful relationship. In that case, somewhere, you are in sacrifice.

Many, if not all of us, went into sacrifice as children. At the core of abuse and dysfunction in families is the dynamic of children sacrificing themselves for their parents, for the good of the family. As we know, children react when their parents are fighting or divorcing. They might act out by getting into trouble (subconsciously to distract their parents from fighting each other), or become really good students or quiet and withdrawn. These are all acts of sacrifice, when children give up their lives, their essential selves, to try and make things right within their family. To some extent, we all became, at least for a while, the child our parents wanted, and we often took on many of their issues.

Client Story:

Lucy came for marriage counselling and her story was, sadly, a common one; she had been married 15 years and felt like she had no life of her own. She spent her time taking care of her two children, then making sure that when her husband came home his needs were taken care of too. She was toying with the idea of leaving the marriage and finding a life for herself.

I explained this was not a good idea for it was only a matter of time before she found another situation where she felt she had no life of her own. Finishing this marriage would not deal with the problem. If she took this route, she would either never go back into a meaningful relationship, or she would start another one and find herself back in the same situation in a short period of time.

We did some regression therapy and she went back to the time when her mother had been hospitalised for six months, and she felt she could no longer be the carefree little girl. At the time, she made the subconscious choice to give up her dreams and passions in order to take care of her father and two brothers. She had learned to put everyone else before herself and now she was repeating this pattern with her husband and children.

Lucy understood that she could follow her dreams and have a relationship based on sharing, rather than sacrifice. She therefore learned the greatest of all relationship lessons: how to be in a relationship and have your own life!

Usually, at some point, we get tired of the sacrifice. So we rebel, run away or leave home. That then becomes the pattern for how we end future relationships; we make others wrong until they are wrong enough and then we can leave, become independent and do whatever we want when we want. And we call that freedom! But when we go back into a relationship later in our lives it will have the same dynamics as going back into our family. Oops. We haven't broken free at all, we are just re-running the same old patterns.

✓ Try this:

Remember that wishful feeling, that dream of having a perfect family Christmas? You arrive laden with presents, determined to have a loving, harmonious time with your parents and siblings. How long does that last? No matter how good your intentions, no matter how much deep breathing you do, they all start driving you crazy and you are mortified to realise that you are feeling and acting like a five-year-old again. How long before you find an excuse to escape, until that feeling of relief when you have them in your rear view mirror? It is similar, sometimes, to that relief you feel when you end a relationship. On the surface there are tears but underneath there is that overwhelming feeling of relief: *'Thank goodness I have got my life back. Hooray! Now it's just me and the open road.'*

Be honest with yourself, when did you last have that feeling either in your present relationship or in your last one?

The other compensatory behaviour to sacrifice is to go into indulgence. The sacrifice-indulgence dynamic happens throughout the power struggle too and has similarities to the anorexic-bulimic complex. In order to be good and loveable (glossy magazine model slim) you starve yourself to the point where it is so unbearable you lose control and binge on your forbidden foods. The guilt this induces makes you feel so bad, you starve yourself even further. It is only a matter of time before your so-called 'willpower' gives way to another binge and the vicious spiral continues.

When we feel we have sacrificed ourselves we feel compelled to compensate. For example, let's say a woman who learned to be a 'people pleaser' as a child, who has given up her needs to that of her family, has spent all day cooking, cleaning and looking after boisterous children. Her relationship is in the dead zone and she feels exhausted and irritable keeping up the 'happy family' front. When her partner returns home grumpy, critical and unappreciative of her efforts, it is no surprise she feels the urge to spend the evening eating cake and the next day impulse shopping on credit cards – the evidence of which she will probably hide from her partner. The guilt she feels about this just keeps the spiral dynamic going.

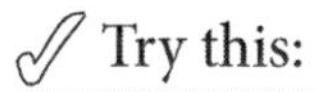

The first step out of the sacrifice-indulgent spiral is simply becoming aware that you are in this cycle. Maybe your relationship has polarised with one partner acting out the indulgence and the other caught in the sacrifice position. Once you have this awareness, the next step is to recognise the reason you have caught yourself like this. It is because you are frightened of taking the next step in some area of your life.

Naturally people caught in this trap look at you as if you are totally heartless if you dare suggest to them such a scenario. But usually a few moments of honest research will bring you to the same conclusion. So now it is about facing your fear and being willing to move forward. That is what it takes; you don't consciously need to know what the step is you just need to have the courage to take it. The rest will be handled when you are open to it.

Dead Zone Stage Trap 3: Competition

We live in a society where competition is encouraged, but as far as relationships go it can be deadly. It is a stage we all need to experience and work through but not to get caught in.

One of the purposes of a relationship is to learn to give and receive – not to take – and therefore find happiness and also success, as both happiness and success go hand in hand. How this giving and receiving works is a bit like this:

Let's face it, nobody wants to live with the same person for any length of time. If you woke up and saw exactly the same person every day you would quickly lose the will to live. So what do we do? What we do is give to our partner in every possible way (without going into sacrifice) because everybody changes when we give to them. As we give to them they blossom, they beam back at us. What is really going on when our partner starts to fail, starts looking a little down? Then it means that instead of giving you have started to compete, possibly at a subconscious level, but you are playing win-lose, rather than win-win.

Competition is destructive to relationships because competition is based on a belief in the dynamic of win-lose, we win and someone else loses, rather than equality. And win-lose is based on a belief in scarcity, that there is not enough to go around. The concept of scarcity started for us when we were very small, when we learned to compete even with our closest family to get the attention and love we craved. Even today, if you are competitive in your workplace you will carry that into your home, into your bedroom and into your children's lives.

Many of us hide our competitive nature but we can often see the effects of it on the people closest to us. We can remember that if a close friend or relative is not doing well and not looking good, then in some way we are winning the competition. But we will not get away unscathed. We might win but we will still have to pay in some way; maybe by having to care for them, pay for them, or by being left to pick up the pieces of their shattered lives. There are no winners in this kind of competition.

✓ Try this:

If someone around you is failing, you may be tempted to ignore them, wish they would change, or complain about them. Instead, focus on how you could support them. You might give them a call, send a card, or simply bring them to mind and bless them. When you give your support you not only help them, you also heal a level of your competition.

How can competing with others be what life is about? We are all different and we can never see the whole picture of what is going on for someone else. It is about being our shining self, whatever that looks like, being the best we can be and supporting others to be the best they can be.

Dead Zone Stage Trap 4: Fear of the Next Step

There is a basic psychology within us fallible human beings that makes us fear change, fear taking the next step in our lives. Doing the 'same old, same old' is what keeps us stuck in the dead zone and makes us unattractive to our partner – as well as making our partner seem unattractive to us.

Typically we go through life moving from one step to the next but at some point we start to fear that change, that movement forward. So how do we subconsciously stop ourselves moving on? We create a problem to get caught up and stuck in – and not many problems come bigger than being embroiled in a big power struggle with someone, or being stuck in the dead zone and feeling like a failure.

It is natural to fear the unknown, to be scared about moving into unchartered waters. And here lies the rub, because we have been sold the myth that hooking up with our 'true love' means we will live happily ever after. We somehow think that when we've arrived at happiness there is nothing else to do but lie back and enjoy it all. But life and relationships aren't like that. Happy partners are those who grow and evolve together. The only constant in life is change – and change can be scary.

At its most basic level fear really comes down to the belief that we will lose something; and this is how it appears at this stage. In fact, the only thing we really lose is our control. What we get in return for giving up our control is far more valuable than staying stuck. But that means embracing the insecurity that comes from stepping outside our comfort zone.

In return for giving up our control we gain partnership, which brings more intimacy and success in all areas of our lives. The natural corollary to giving up control is finding interdependence and partnership. Now how scary are these payoffs, really? Aren't they the things we all yearn for? Not only does giving up control mean we gain deeper intimacy and more worldly success, we also start to win our heart back; things start meaning more to us, we are more moved, touched and become more responsive to those around us.

Hundreds of clients have said to us at this point: '*OK, show me the next step and I will take it.*' But that is not the way it works. Even if we did tell you the next step, you still would not take it. You might think about it a lot. You might even think it sounds like a great idea, but with your current level of control you would not take it. To get through the dead zone, we need to learn the scariest of all lessons (especially for independent people), we need to learn to surrender. That does not mean we need to lie down and let others walk all over us – that is sacrifice. In true surrender, we give up being right about the things we think we are right about. We go back to being a good student, of learning to learn again – and we can't learn when we think we are right and know it all.

✓ Try this:

To have the courage to move forward, what you need most is to become willing. Willingness opens your mind and starts the learning process. When you become willing, whatever you need to change – the book, the friend, the job – and whatever you need to accomplish will become clear. The next step will move towards you. Once you are ready the next step will become clear.

Imagine that you stand at a crossroads. One of the choices facing you will take you in a whole new direction. The other is the familiar choice you have always made.

Imagine that you make this familiar choice again. Where will it take you and what will your life look like in six months? In one year? Do you recognise that you have been at this point before? In fact, can you see that this step circles back until you are at the same crossroads again? How does it feel to make the familiar, safe choice?

Now imagine that you are willing to step out in the new direction. Where might it take you, what might your life look like in six months? In one year? How does it feel to take this step into the unknown?

Would you be willing now to take the new step, and to allow change to happen around you?

There are many traps in the dead zone and many ways to escape it. Maybe the quickest and often the most effective is to have the courage to say what you are thinking, to take an emotional risk and share yourself honestly in some way. When we are in the dead zone we have given everything except the one thing people really want, which is ourselves. We have given our roles and duties and a wide selection of cardboard cutouts but not ourselves: ourselves and our secrets, our fears, our broken pieces, our real feelings about ourselves or simply US.

OUR STORY: Coming Out of the Dead Zone

Sue says:

On our first visit to the dead zone, which was before we separated for two years, I was trying to hold it all together and pretend everything was OK – even though it clearly wasn't. After we reunited and went through the honeymoon and power struggle phases again, our second visit to the dead zone was only a matter of time. This time though, we decided to tackle it head on. We committed to being completely honest with each other about the issues that were creating distance between us again. We went away on a long camping weekend, just the two of us, took long walks and committed to answering any question the other asked. It brought up many secrets and painful home truths – but it worked and was a huge step in us both becoming truly authentic and relaxed with each other.

We just kept talking and talking, learning about each other all over again. I felt as if I was starting a fresh and fascinating topic. It was amazing that Jeff was also curious about me, so open-minded and uncontrolling that everything felt easy. After about six months we went on holiday to Scotland as a family and Jeff and I finally reunited for good. We decided to tell the children once we had climbed to the top of this beautiful hill and I will never forget their reaction. They were absolutely elated: screaming and hugging us and jumping up and down with delight.

In 1996 Jeff, I and the children, who were then teenagers, did a ceremony in a workshop led by Chuck Spezzano where we retook our marriage vows and made promises as a family to love and care for each other. It was so, so special. We have a big collage of photos from the ceremony on display at home and friends always comment on it – we are all just shining in the pictures.

Jeff says:

When we were first in the dead zone everyone else looked attractive and my life was wracked with temptation. But the more I fell for temptation the more guilty I felt, which meant I became even more distant from Sue. I thought when things started going pear-shaped, that was the time to leave the relationship. Wrong!

What worked in the end was realising that this meant it was time to commit: commit to us, to Sue and to open up and move towards her, rather than run for the hills.

The children were over the moon when Sue and I got back together, but that was when the real work between us began. Being absolutely honest with each other, no matter what, wasn't easy – it was often very painful indeed – and it took a long time for us to trust each other fully.

I had spent such a long time not learning about relationships, such a long time being right about everything, it took a while to remember that I was in a learning situation. And there were lessons almost daily! I had to completely change my attitude to emotional pain, and after years of blame and recrimination I had to resist the temptation to return to those defences. In relationships we will be confronted with every broken piece of our minds and if we defend against this process we will suffer. It was a tough lesson to learn after years of being right: my greatest defence!

Today, I no longer see the independent macho male persona as strong or courageous. It was only by facing up to my relationship problems that I learned what true courage and integrity is. Learning how to really love Sue and always move towards her has been the making of me.

This is the basic pattern of life. We need to be good students for the rest of our lives because we all have so much to learn – and in no place is there more to learn than in our relationships. Once we commit to the power of relationships, and to our continued growth and learning rather than our control, life becomes exciting again. Our partner becomes a source of interest and sustenance again, and we finally step into the partnership stage.

Chapter 7

PARTNERSHIP STAGE

'I want to stand with you on a mountain
I want to bathe with you in the sea
I want to lay like this forever
Until the sun falls down on me.'

Savage Garden

Reaching the partnership stage feels a bit like coming ashore from a shipwreck. After all the storms, turbulence and the worrying: '*Will we make it or will we die here?*' there is the peace and certainty of dry land.

You know you are in partnership when you feel the connection with your partner. We call this interdependence. For the most part you are aware of the dance of independence-dependence and you recognise the pitfalls and know the ways through. Your partner no longer seems like an adversary, out to trip you up and gloat over your failures. They no longer seem like a complete let-down; your relationship no longer feels threatened by the next big bust-up. You feel like you are on the same team, as equals, and that you can be honest about how you feel and face difficult times together. You recognise each other's strengths and weaknesses and it feels like there is nothing to fear because the teamwork – the interdependence and the equality – will prevail. So you have the confidence to take more risks – and every time you do so, the partnership strengthens.

If you have been on business team-building exercises or sporting teams you know how this dynamic of interdependence is what coaches are working towards, so that the team or the business can take risks, can 'think outside the box' and 'get in the zone.' It is the same in our intimate relationship.

Interdependence & Interconnection

Most of us are a combination of dependent and independent characteristics within our relationship, which changes over time. As we have seen, the dynamic always has to balance itself out somehow. This is why there is absolutely no point trying to make your partner change into who you think they should be, believing that only then will you be happy. As you can see from our story, it only takes one. When one person changes and moves forward in their life, so does the other.

OUR STORY: Our Energetic Interconnection

Sue says:

I see now that Jeff was the one who had the courage to call it a day on our dysfunctional relationship. Not that he had any positive suggestions other than 'this is not working,' but I could have gone on forever playing the same dependent role, not daring to end it and take my next step. Our extreme imbalance and the break-up forced me to face my feelings of failure in my two marriages, and once I stopped being right about all men being 'unfaithful bastards', I could recognise my part in those disasters. Only then did true partnership become a real possibility.

Jeff says:

> When Sue let go of her dependence on me, suddenly, even though I was 4,000 miles away, I could no longer play the independent one. I could not dissociate from my feelings anymore. She could talk and plead and beg with me all she wanted (and indeed, she did, many times), but only when she changed herself did I change. In fact, I was forced to change. The feelings I had locked up for so long came in wave after wave. I realised how emotionally brave and strong she must have been to 'hold' those feelings for me all that time. But letting go of them was the best gift she could have given me – because, eventually, it brought me back to myself. These events remain one of the most powerful experiences of my life.

When things like this happen to you, you reassess your whole worldview. In this time of science, we tend to look for rational proof of things – we want proof to be tangible, even physical. For the most part we don't value the unseen forces around us. Relationships are an energetic exchange that continues no matter whether the person is physically present with you or not.

We have seen this time and again with our workshop participants; when people make a big internal shift, they often later report that their partner or close family members magically change too. When we heal, we heal together.

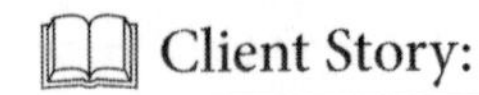

Client Story:

When Janet stopped needing her mother to apologise for her critical behaviour, and instead apologized to her mother for her own antagonism, she was amazed that her mother was able to admit her feelings of inadequacy. Martin let go of expecting his dinosaur Head of Department to change and suddenly his boss was seeking his opinion on how to modernize. Zarah was forever covering for her husband's alcoholism; when she took the next step in her own life, in this case finding a job, he started to ask for help and joined Alcoholics Anonymous.

We never heal alone. We are all indelibly interconnected. Often during a seminar we are asked, *'How do I know I have changed?'* and the short answer is another question. When you go back out into your life are the significant people in your life different? Do *they* appear to have changed? If the answer is yes then so have you changed, and if the answer is no then there is more to do.

Client Story:

Jenny was attending a 2-day seminar in London where she had been so confronted that she left at the end of the first day in a rage. This rage was strengthened when she got home to find her partner had left a note saying he had decided to visit his family in the north of England. The following morning in the seminar she let out her rage and complained bitterly about his impromptu action.

We explained that it was understandable considering her state that he had taken the course of self-preservation, because it was obvious she had been spoiling for a fight. During the morning we worked through her source of rage and did a commitment exercise with her partner. She wrote to me later to say she had been delighted to return home and find he was there to welcome her and they had reached a new level of partnership. It was apparent that her partner was tuned into her state and responded accordingly!

We don't ask that you believe what we say, but how about doing your own research?

✓ Try this:

Think of something that is bothering you right now in your family life or your relationship; something that you worry about, or a recent upset. What could you change within yourself rather than trying to change the other person or the situation? What attitude or demand could you really change internally? What step could you take in your own life that would take the pressure out of the dynamic?

When you commit to your change and implement it, without expecting anything in return, simply notice how others around you change. When you do it right, it works out right. You will get instant feedback, one way or the other.

Love *Can* Last A Lifetime

Partnership can be strong enough to last a lifetime but only if you are both willing to embrace change – real inner change, not just superficial outer changes. Life is constantly evolving and happy couples constantly evolve too. No one wants to be married to someone who never evolves or changes, who is the same person for thirty years. What makes you truly attractive to each other is the vibrancy of growing and developing together. Only then do you become true-life partners.

Remember, the purpose of having relationships is to learn to give and receive. As we give to our partners they grow and surprise us. When we stop giving, our partners appear to stop growing and changing. Our giving is what makes our relationships work. If we want a 100% partner then we need to become a 100% partner, and we do that by giving at greater and greater levels. This takes honesty, courage, determination, willingness and commitment. It is not an easy path. But when we do bust through a set of old subconscious patterns together, the pay-off is that we come back into harmony and into a new honeymoon phase. And the difference in the partnership stage is this: even when new issues arise again, you know you are on the same team; it is not a chance to gloat or blame.

Relationships end when one partner gets to an issue that they're unable to work through, for whatever reason. When one partner is unable to follow the other in their personal evolution then couples often split amicably, knowing that they have simply outgrown each other. Love really can last a lifetime, whether it's as partners or as friends.

We make it sound so simple don't we? Well, of course, love relationships are nowhere near as straightforward as our common cultural myths about love have led us to believe. But once we have worked through these stages of relationship, we will be rewarded by having a true partner, a true friend, lover, wife or husband and life companion. These are the rewards of our willingness to work through all of the thousands of traps we have in our minds. This transformation is never about time, it is about courage; the courage to be wrong about what you are convinced you are right about; the courage to have true intimacy with another; the courage to quit the fights and believe only in love, again and again and again.

OUR STORY: Living in Partnership

Sue says:

In the twenty years since Jeff and I got back together, we have taken faltering steps towards more and more partnership. I feel more equal, I appreciate him more, and our relationship feels more intimate, more real. We work together as Psychology of Vision trainers, bringing different flavours into our business. Sometimes I pinch myself and wonder how it all happened; how we now travel abroad together to amazing places and help people with their relationships; how this barely-dreamed of level of personal happiness has become my reality; how our children can finally witness and celebrate a growing relationship. We still face times of inequality and uncertainty, of independence and dependence, and there's no doubt that doing the work we do helps us stay on course and live the principles of partnership. As the saying goes, 'we teach what we most need to learn.'

Jeff says:

At first, I was challenged by co-facilitating seminars with Sue. I was so used to giving seminars by myself, I had to consciously choose to include her and learn that lesson all men need to learn: 'Slow down!' I certainly needed to be aware of which way we were headed. Every situation was fraught with the chance we would both charge off in opposite directions. What made it safe was our willingness to connect our minds and hearts as closely as possible before a section, resist the temptation to be right about anything and most importantly: Listen!

Today I am in a constant state of admiration when working with Sue and I know what she brings to the relationship and to the work makes us far more than the sum of each of us.

Part Three:

SEX & AFFAIRS

'It's the heart afraid of breaking that never learns to dance.'

Bette Midler

At its best, sex is restorative, revitalising and deepens our connection with our partner. Beyond the plumbing, it is another form of communication available to us, another way of giving love to our partner. Sadly, however, it is also the most wounded area of the human psyche – and in many ways we are all, collectively, still recovering from many hundreds of years of sexuality being labelled dirty and sinful by major religions.

After years of conducting seminars around the world we have heard thousands of stories about sexual abuse. Once people are willing to get honest it seems there are very few who have not experienced some form of sexual abuse as children, either from siblings, other family members, close friends or total strangers, paedophiles or carers. It seems to go from generation to generation.

Needless to say, most of us totally repressed these experiences but now they show up in our lives as either obsession with sex, usually in the form of pornography, or as the opposite: lack of passion and prudishness.

As one of the most wounded parts of us, our sexuality will become an issue that needs to be addressed and communicated about during every mature and growing relationship. Sex can become a battleground – or it can be a place of fun and pleasure, of healing and sanctuary, of rejuvenation and loving. The choice is ours. If we are willing to learn to communicate, especially to communicate lovingly about what is not working, sex can keep a relationship growing because in itself it is such a great channel of communication. Our sexuality is an area in which all of us can feel a failure at times, even the greatest stud. So we need to be vigilant, willing to face and talk about it.

There is great energy in our sexuality. Yet most of us have grown up to fear it, to repress it or hide it in some way because we know the damage it can cause to our relationships when it is out of control. But what keeps sexual energy safe is love. Sometimes, the simplest advice to a sexless couple is just to lie together in bed and love each other the best they can, and then let the rest take care of itself – because sex at its best is simply an expression of love.

Chapter 8

SEX THROUGH THE STAGES

Our sexuality goes through stages, just as our relationships do. Ideally, we have no judgment about each stage, and nor do we camp out too long in any one of them – until the last one that is, the partnership stage.

Honeymoon Sex

It starts with the 'kid in the candy store' energy of the romantic honeymoon stage. After years of being told not to, being unable to or holding back, all of a sudden we can have it all. Then everything is right with the world as we taste the sweetness that is sex. You and your partner can't take your hands off each other and your stomach does that funny flippy thing each time you think of all the naughtiness you have been up to all weekend. As much as we want this stage to last forever, just like the honeymoon itself, it is only a matter of time before it burns out.

After this stage we progress to the generic kind of sex. Sex becomes the goal and it does not matter about who the other person is, provided they do the business. Many of us never get past this stage because it is basically about getting our needs meet. We are making love for the sake of sex and our satisfaction, rather than making it about the other person. In this stage sex can become objectified; we make our partner an object for our satisfaction rather than the experience of joining and communion. Recently, we have started to work in Asia and often hear stories of couples who have sex without any foreplay or cuddling or kissing, they just do it!

But for a living, loving, working relationship, we need to move on to the next stage where we start making love to the person for who they are. Then at later stages we make love to their essence, which in truth is also ours. The act of sex then becomes tantric or transcendental. It really does become an earth-moving *'Oh God! Oh God!'* religious type of experience.

Never base a relationship solely on pleasure, for as the old saying goes: *'Those who seek pleasure will find pain.'* But having and enjoying things that give you pleasure is natural. In fact when we have the sexual aspect of life balanced there are many other benefits. When your sexual energy is expressed and centred, it gives you zest for life and the courage to go for your dreams – not to mention a twinkle in your eye and a 'cat that got the cream' smile on your face. We feel more fulfilled and as we venture out into the world we feel braver. The reason for this is that sexual energy, when it is in the flow, is the same energy that gives us drive in our lives. It gives us the 'balls' to face challenges and not give up. We feel fearless and focused and are not easily stopped. When we feel loved and cherished through the intimacy of sex, we also stimulate all the deep feelings that make up love like sharing, appreciation, generosity, tenderness and compassion to name a few. With this wind in our sails we become truly heroic.

Power Struggle Sex

In the power struggle stage, sex so easily becomes part of the battleground. One partner might act out the dependent side, being needy around sex, feeling the emotions. Meanwhile, the other partner acts out the independent side – experiencing the temptations and feeling dissociated. If the polarisation gets too great, then the relationship is in danger and one partner or the other needs to bridge the difference.

Often we find that a man who is independent in other ways can be dependent sexually. If you are a woman (or man) who knowingly uses sex to punish your otherwise independent partner, give it up as best you can for the sake of the relationship. Sex is a great weapon to use when you want to attack your partner in some way *but* you lose a vital route back to true communication and partnership. One partner may try hard to communicate and when this fails, as it often seems to, they then withdraw sexually, that being the only card they believe they have left - but sex is also the one thing that might have motivated change and been a way of getting their attention.

Generally, men are more likely to feel loved through sex, and women are more likely to feel loved through romance, through being valued and cared for. This difference, if it exists, can also become polarised.

Sue says:

> Before we split up, I had this tactic of keeping Jeff talking when we were in bed and I knew he wanted to make love. I felt I finally had his attention and boy was I going to make use of it! So I would ask lots of questions and ramble on about my day, despite his impatience. It was a form of control because I got the communication I craved, almost as a prior condition. Of course my efforts to manipulate in all the wrong ways also killed any spontaneity and fun, and pushed us further towards the dead zone.

Usually, at some point, our relationship polarises so that in one partner the sexual energy becomes exaggerated. That partner spends a lot of time thinking about sex and talking about sex – or the lack of it. Their seeking of pleasure may spill over to other aspects of life, like food or drink, where this appetite for pleasure and indulgence becomes, at times, obsessive. And sexually they become the prurient one looking at the opposite sex with that 'just got out of jail' look.

The other partner balances them out and becomes the prude. He or she can live as a monk or a nun and go for years without even a conscious thought of sex. If they take it too far, the prude will not take pleasure in anything, not even a great sunset. Sometimes this partner seeks a higher path and becomes very 'spiritual' and pretends to rise above such base things as sex.

In some cases people live these two aspects out in their own lives. They may spend the first 20 years in the exaggerated position and then suddenly switch and give up sex and live as a prude. Usually these people are single!

As every relationship balances, one partner can correct this imbalance and come back to their centre where sex again becomes natural, becomes healing and finally becomes transcendental. Being aware of the imbalance is key, as well as avoiding blaming or fighting. You will know when you have truly taken the centre because your partner will very soon join you in this place – and then the celebrations can commence.

On our way to happiness we need to work through every judgment we have until we come to a place of acceptance and peace about everything. You may have already experienced what we call 'the shadow trap' (see Part Two, page 65) within the power struggle stage, when our partner suddenly takes on all the sexual characteristics of our worst nightmare. Maybe they remind us of Lester the Molester, or they seem to have become a prude, or be totally uninspiring in some way. What has happened here is that a shadow aspect of ourselves, something we judged in ourselves and repressed at some distant time, has resurfaced for healing in the guise of our partner.

Another possibility in this shadow trap is for one partner to start believing they are in some way the toxic man or toxic woman, and that somehow being close to their partner will cause them harm. Mostly this is a subconscious and hidden belief, but as it flits through a partner's mind it results in them not totally giving themselves during sex or at other times of intimacy.

Client Story:

Brett and Elisabeth were obviously in love. They seemed the perfect couple and everyone who knew them felt the same. I met them in a seminar in Canada and they lit people up with new faith that they too could find true love.

When I returned a year later they were in the throes of splitting up. It was a shock and I was pleased when Elisabeth asked for a coaching session. On a conscious level she was heartbroken and certainly did not understand fully what was going on. During our session we got to a belief she was toxic. This belief had started for her very early in life when her mother had fallen sick and Elisabeth thought that it was her fault: there was some quality about her that had caused her mother's illness and she was therefore toxic to anyone who got close to her.

She had repressed this belief and now was sub-consciously pushing her partner away, not because she did not love him but because she believed she would hurt him in some way. After this insight and then changing her beliefs they were soon back into a new honeymoon.

Awareness is important in dealing with any polarisation, and recognising when this dynamic starts to show itself. Communicating with your partner about what you are feeling and what you want is also key and once again it is time to move towards your partner. Don't settle for any polarisation and recognise that fighting around sex never helps in any relationship.

✓ Try this:

Firstly, agree a time. Make a date to sit and talk and then during the communication remember a no-blame, no-fault attitude is best. Keep in mind that any blame, any use of the word 'you' is not recommended, because the instant blame is used, the fight is only a matter of time away. During the communication, speak of your own experience, what works for you and what does not. It is OK to communicate about your needs but not to develop any expectations your partner will take care of them. Speak of how you feel and take responsibility for these feelings, which means you recognise these feelings were most likely within you long before you met your partner. Use the communication as a way of clearing what is between you and your partner and regard it as a joining, a coming together which if done well will result in a mental, emotional and physical joining.

When you become good at communicating, you have the first step in any significant change, as communication is the essential ingredient for change. Often people say that their partner is not open with them, they withhold stuff, but whatever they are doing, so are you. You must get past any messages in your mind such as, *'I can't open up because then I will get attacked'*, or *'if I give you an inch you'll take a mile'*, or *'I'll only surrender after you have'*. These are all strategies that guarantee poor communication and the continuation of the power struggle. Have the courage to say how you are feeling and what is going on for you, not to hold anything back, and if you do that while taking total responsibility, your partner will listen and at some point will say 'me too' about their feelings. At this point comes the recognition that both parties in any fight are actually felling the same. Now you are building bridges past the divide of two people just feeling a bad feeling and the resulting power struggle.

Sex is about communication and at its best is a truly healing and even enlightening path, and at the worst it is about power and abuse. Take a moment and ask yourself - what was it that you were communicating the last time you had sex?

Dead Zone Sex

The dead zone is, as we have seen, the place where the spark goes out. Usually when we first enter the dead zone we feel that we need to experiment sexually more and more. In the dead zone, our ability to feel has been reduced, so we become kinkier, in order just to feel something. We spice things up by using pornography or a variety of sex toys. Needless to say, at some point even this is no longer enough and the sex dies. Or we do it just because we feel it is our duty, or our role, to do it.

We certainly don't believe that your sex life should only be about the missionary position. It is healthy to experiment and enjoy variety. But it is important not to turn your partner into an object and to remember that sex is an expression of love.

In our work, it is common to speak with people – usually men – who complain about the lack of sex in their relationship. Our first question to them is: 'So, how come you don't want sex?' They naturally think we have gone deaf and repeat their complaint more loudly. But still we keep the same question running until at some point they start to reflect upon it. Then, invariably, out of their subconscious will come an event in their youth when they made a choice to give up on sex, because of their guilt regarding something they did that they were ashamed of in some way.

Client Story:

Mike had a history of disastrous relationships when it came to sex. He had an obvious pattern of starting passionate, steamy relationships but then he would start to withdraw and finally shut down. We accessed Mike's intuition by asking him intentionally vague questions that bypass the conscious mind. This intuitive method connects to the subconscious and unconscious mind and we then ask the participant to listen to their intuition rather than listen to their memory. The answers that come in lead us back to past incidents.

In this way we traced Mike's sexual guilt back to an incident when he was a small boy crawling around the kitchen floor while his mother was cooking. At one point he crawled under her dress, looked up and had a reaction to what he saw. His mother, because of her sexual guilt, also had a strong reaction. The guilt and resulting belief system he carried away from this incident was enough to play havoc with his adult relationships. Once he cleared this up and realised he had nothing to feel guilty about, he went on to enjoy a new, deep and loving relationship.

In the grand scheme of things, this childhood memory seems like a minor incident compared to the damage it caused in his later life. But in our experience it is not the trauma that creates the negative patterns, but the choices that were made at the time. The subconscious childhood choices we make about ourselves, our family and our world become the software of our lives.

✓ Try this:

All of us have these places, these guilty secrets, and they call for forgiveness. Mostly we were very young children who were experimenting with life. We certainly didn't do anything that deserves punishment and withdrawal, and we need to go back to these incidents and make new decisions, new choices and then close the distance that guilt creates.

We know that it might be strange to think about changing what is past but this is a perfect time to use the Iceberg model on page 34, Chapter 3. Our past is a story in our minds and we can go back using this model, and change the perspective we previously chose and the new perspective will change our belief system and therefore our feelings and behaviours. This is especially true with guilt as guilt calls for correction and for learning, not for punishment.

When we feel guilty we withdraw, and when we withdraw one of the first things to go is our sexuality. We might leave a cardboard cutout of ourself in the bed – but we will still be thinking about the garden, the shopping or the new job.

It is also common to hear stories of people having a great sex life until they get married (ah marriage, that great contraceptive). This pattern, similar to that in the last section, often shows up for people who have led a very promiscuous life until about the age of forty, when, somehow, the tap gets turned off and that is it. Typically driven by feelings of guilt, they withdraw. Even if they have sex, it feels like a sacrifice – a duty or a role. Feeling that sex is a burden rather than a pleasure, brings little satisfaction and further distances couples, one from the other. Again, this situation requires communication, authenticity and honesty.

✓ Try this:

When working with couples in a committed relationship who want to revive or rebalance their sex lives, we suggest this exercise: For one week one partner does exactly what the other partner wants, they totally surrender to them. Then the following week they reverse the arrangement. It is a great way of learning about your partner and also working through your judgments and hang-ups.

Needless to say this is an exercise for a couple in a long-term relationship who trust each other, and have found themselves in the dead zone. It is a way of taking risks that will get you out of the deadness, emotional risks in this case expressed through sex. What creates the dead zone is a distance between each partner and this is a method of closing that distance by surrendering and making the relationship more important than your defences. It is an exercise in communication and understanding not an exercise in domination or abuse.

Recognise that if there is a fear of how your partner might behave then you need to clear some more basic issues before doing this exercise, or certainly communicate about your concerns before you start.

The Oedipal Complex

One of the biggest traps to show up in the dead zone stage of sex is the Oedipal Complex. This is where we project onto our partner any unfinished areas of our early sexual attraction towards our parent of the opposite sex – and the resulting guilt.

Understanding the effect of the Oedipal myth on all our lives was the genius of Freud. In years of working at depth in the mind, Chuck Spezzano confirmed this myth has a profound effect on just about everyone. Originating in early childhood, Oedipal attractions emerge when, in the world of scarcity or fighting in our unbonded family, we seek love and nurturing from the individual to whom we are most drawn. In the worst cases, this gets acted out in families as incest, but few of us escape its effects. The Oedipal trap, well known in psychology, stays hidden until we have spent time in the dead zone.

Most of us have no conscious memory of this early sexual attraction with our parent of the opposite sex, but the psychological effects are numerous. It shows up on a conscious level in relationships in the following ways:

- No relationships
- Deadness in relationships
- Fighting for no or little reason
- Triangle relationships (recreating the original family triangle)
- Feeling of revulsion around our bodies or our partner's body, especially during sex
- In business, it shows up as creating success then suddenly losing everything, then again building up your business, reaching success and then crashing again and again.

All these are indicators that Oedipus is alive and well in our subconscious mind. Just as most of us, in our original families, turned away from any unresolved sexual attractions, we now turn away from our partner – and so we bring emotional and sexual deadness into our partnership. When you consider that a large percentage of relationships fail because of these dynamics, it is important not to underestimate the effects of the Oedipal urge on our everyday lives.

✓ Try this:

The way through this Oedipal trap is commitment. Your partner is not your parent, and when we daily choose our partner and commit to them at every opportunity, in every possible way, we can springboard from the dead zone into a fresh and rewarding partnership.

Are you willing to make your present relationship more important than whatever occurred in your past? Will you recognise the power and courage of commitment and, in the face of everything, still choose to commit and move towards your partner in the knowledge that they are not your father or mother?

Partnership Sex

There is a saying amongst tantra teachers that: '*Women come to sex through love and men come to love through sex.*' We believe this to be true. As we have already said, it is our experience that men tend to feel loved by sex, whereas women tend to feel loved when they are being listened to and romanced.

Nothing turns a woman on more than feeling that she is being heard and is respected for herself, not only for her body. In fact, one of the biggest aphrodisiacs for women is when men overtly appreciate them and what they do.

In the partnership stage, both people recognise and appreciate their different 'turn-ons', whatever they might be. We think it was Sigmund Freud who said, '*the only form of unnatural sex is no sex*'. Our sexual energy is a natural part of our life force, one that adds juiciness and flow to our lives.

The essence of sex is communication and it can therefore be useful to look at it purely from this aspect. Sex driven by the sole desire to get one's needs met is predicated on selfishness. When his or her needs are satisfied, that partner closes down. This kind of sex is inevitably one-sided, and can lead to one partner craving more and more sex but becoming less and less fulfilled. Furthermore, when our sex life is in the dead zone we can even become disassociated from our needs, which can result in craving increasingly kinky and extreme forms of sex, just in order to feel something. No longer satisfied by straight sex, we resort to fantasy or deviance to spice up the experience. Based on needs, however, we are never truly satisfied by our sexual encounters and finally we give up.

When we communicate genuine passion, the experience becomes wholly satisfying. We are able to communicate not only passion, but love and intimacy, at greater and deeper levels. Our lovemaking becomes freer and more fulfilling because we are free from the guilt and belief systems associated with sex.

When your sex life is no longer an area of power struggle or dead zone where it feels routine or boring, you don't need to demand more and more kinkiness from your partner in order to feel anything. For the most part the energy that's driving sex is not neediness or demands, but rather two people giving of themselves to each other.

In the partnership stage you no longer have any feelings of repulsion about the act of sex, about your body or about your partner's body. You have worked through many of your negative beliefs and judgments about sex, sexuality and the opposite sex. The sexual act is really about the essence of the other person; it is not about their body, it's not your idea of what sex should be, how long for, or any gymnastics. You are willing to cater to each other's tastes and needs.

It's not that issues don't need discussion and communication, but you do keep moving towards each other. Sex is an expression of communication, love, friendship and equality. And it's an act of passion that does not diminish; an act of surrender by both parties that allows energy and grace to flow through you and your union. You both recognise and appreciate how sex adds flow to your life, a juiciness that lubricates life and is part of the whole picture of feeling alive and connected through each other to nature. As an expression of sexual energy and life force, sex is fun and natural.

OUR STORY: Partnership Sex

Jeff says:

In my worst moments during our break-up, if anyone had told me I would find Sue sexually attractive again, I would have just laughed. I certainly found other people sexually attractive, but the thought of sex with Sue was a non-event. But after I had worked through my independence and won my heart back, it was like finding a new partner. The first time we made love after our separation was truly poetic, absolutely heartfelt and one of the most uplifting moments of my life. Naturally, I have slipped back into my stuff but not nearly as far as I was before and now I always have in mind my goal, which is to repeat that and more. It showed me that sex wasn't about the physical, but rather all about the emotion and the exchange of love.

Chapter 9

WHY PEOPLE HAVE AFFAIRS

Many people believe that affairs destroy a relationship. It is also true that leaving the top off the toothpaste can end a relationship but affairs have a special place in our minds. Yet what we believe is no issues are love-proof. Relationships can survive anything – even affairs.

The most common cause of affairs is when a relationship polarises into the dependent-independent dynamic. One partner becomes dependent and, as we all know, when someone becomes dependent and emotionally clingy, no matter how they look physically, they do become unattractive. They cease to be charismatic, they are most likely burdened with problems and feeling every emotion except the one they should, the one they're avoiding. They start to try and take from their partner and they use their emotions as a lure; instead of dealing with the deeper emotions, they use their partner as a kind of comfort blanket to try to feel better about themselves. However this never works.

The extent to which one partner becomes dependent, the other partner becomes independent. Then, when the independent partner looks at his or her partner they don't see their partner. Instead, they see their worst nightmare – the type of needy person that they swore they would never be like. When you look at it this way, it is no wonder they are tempted to run. So the independent one pulls right back and starts looking around and, of course, becomes tempted. Most of us believe the purpose of temptation is to fall for it and, when we do, the affairs start and we are caught in the trap. The guilt builds and the distance grows.

OUR STORY: Having Affairs

Jeff says:

Even after we got married, I never saw myself as a full time husband and soon fell back into my womanising, philandering ways. I would be at home for a few months, then off working on ships and yachts for months at a time. I thought I loved my independence but the reality was I was totally disconnected from my feelings and terrified to truly commit.

Looking back I was living a lie that I didn't need anyone. I couldn't ask for help and tended to push people away; and that's what I started doing to Sue. When the super-independent me looked at her, I saw a dependent, nagging and unattractive needy person, exactly my worst nightmare. No wonder the grass always looked greener away from home.

Sue says:

It was about five years into our marriage, when the children had come along, that I suspected Jeff was having affairs. But I didn't really want to know about it. It suited me to remain oblivious. I enjoyed being my own boss while he was away on sailing jobs; I had the ring on my finger and the money coming in. To add to the surface impression of a capable independent woman, I was running my own educational publishing business part time. But emotionally I was the typical dependent woman and this soon

> showed up once he was home again. I fell into the cycle of trying to take from Jeff the approval I craved, and had craved all my life. If only he would give it to me, by loving me the way I thought he should, I could feel more attractive and be my old alluring self again.
>
> It was always great to see Jeff at first, but then we would start arguing and it would be a relief when he left. Once again we could avoid dealing with our independent – dependent polarization.

When it comes to affairs, the first impulse is to blame the one who went outside the relationship. But after years of working with couples we have learned a number of things. Firstly, the reason someone has an affair is because they are looking for something that is missing in their marriage.

Let's take the example of someone who doesn't feel loved or nurtured or understood (remembering everyone acts because of how they feel). They then perceive those caring qualities that they miss in another. They become attracted and, step-by-step, walk straight into the trap. Now, remember that every relationship is in balance and having an affair is basically about taking; seeing some quality outside yourself and taking it. Well, the dependent partner is doing exactly the same thing: their dependency is created because they want to take the very same quality from their partner. That is what makes a person dependent; believing that there is something someone else has that they can take. The independent partner in this case is tempted outside the relationship by the very quality their dependent partner is trying to take from them, like understanding or nurturing. Since the independent partner doesn't believe they have what their partner is trying to take from them, they feel like a failure and independent people do not like feeling like a failure. So where do they want to spend their time? Not with their husband or wife, that is for sure.

OUR STORY: Affairs are Not One Person's Fault

Sue says:

> When I finally acted on my suspicions and realised the true picture of Jeff's affairs, I was mortified and angry. But once I began to understand that I was equally responsible for the relationship, I could admit that I was equally out of integrity but just in a different area. I was using the marriage to prop up a picture of myself as a stupendous wife and mother, looking after the home and kids, but this perfect picture was a sham. The truth is that no one could have come between us if we had had a close relationship – we both allowed the distance between us to grow.

Collusion

This takes us to the second reason for affairs. There is a level of collusion going on between all three people. It can get complicated here, as affairs tend to do, so stay with us as best you can as we explain.

In truth there is a next step available to the couple in the main relationship (let's call them Jack and Jill) and an aspect of that next step is a new gift, a new energy, a new level of intimacy that is possible for them. But there is also a level of fear about this new step that both Jack and Jill feel equally, no matter how it looks on the surface. Then typically one partner, in this case say it is Jack, becomes more dependent and clingy and the other partner, Jill, becomes more independent and therefore tempted by someone outside the relationship.

It appears that the temptation is about some physical or, more rarely, mental quality in the third party (who we'll call John) but that is only on the surface. What the real attraction is about is the belief that some emotional 'hole' within the tempted (Jill) will become filled. If the third party (John) is youthful, then the emotional need might be to feel alive again; if the attraction is a high-flying job, then the emotional need might be for adventure and so it goes on.

The key principle to understand is that the essential behaviour of all three people is taking. Jack, as the dependent partner, is trying to take the same quality from Jill, whether that is adventure or feeling alive again. Even if he appears to be giving in a hundred different ways there is still this buried agenda that Jill fulfils his need. Jill is taking from John in the belief her need will get fulfilled, even if she is not consciously aware of what is driving her temptation. In fact, the level of taking between the couple is always equal even though after an affair is revealed the dependent partner acts the most offended. Equally, all three are afraid of taking the next step within the context of their main relationship.

And John? If he too is part of a couple then he and his partner are playing out in their turn the same dynamic of fear of their next step. If John was just getting ready for a relationship, falling for Jill was only Mrs. 80% in terms of availability – and now all three people are trapped. But this is also what all three people want because of their fear of their next step or level. If John could recognise that, while his new married lover has everything he wants, he could just be aware of the feelings but not act on them, then typically within a few weeks Mrs. 100 % would show up, having all the gifts of Mrs. 80%, but being free and unattached.

Both Jack and Jill are subconsciously searching for the same quality, the same gift but from other people rather than recognising they have, within them, the very quality they are looking for. In order to look for something you must know what it is, and to know what it is means you already have it, even if just in potential. If Jack and Jill had kept their energy within the relationship that quality would have surfaced within one or both of them and could then have been given and shared, thereby moving the relationship to a new level.

As another example, a man might be attracted to a third party by a physical property, say her large breasts; remember it is not about the form but about the energy he needs that he believes will be fulfilled by large breasts. In this case it is not difficult to imagine he is looking for a feeling of being nurtured or understood. If he were to observe the third party, even admire her qualities, but keep his energy within his current relationship, then at some point the feeling of being nurtured and understood will become a reality within that relationship. As he embodies the energy of being nurtured and understood his partner would then receive it and respond. This is the purpose of relationships, to give and to receive. The answer to any scarcity is always to give what you perceive is missing, and what we give is what we get.

All affairs bring consequences. The level of guilt and secrecy that can build up is enough to ensure never being truly happy in a triangle relationship. At some point, the guilt gets too strong and the unfaithful partner eventually leaves some evidence of their activity around – and gets caught. Now there is a choice: Do you take responsibility and heal and learn and sort out this dynamic? Or do you use this to seek revenge, get caught in a fight and then go on and repeat the pattern in your next relationship?

Sometimes it takes something as drastic as an affair to get couples out of the dead zone.

Let's say a woman is married to General Stonewall Jackson, metaphorically speaking. Stonewall Jackson was a general in the American Civil war who got his name for not giving an inch, for being really stubborn and unmoving. In a long-term relationship, which has by now hit the dead zone, the man stays logical and analytical, totally unmoving and devoid of any emotions. For the most part he is dead.

The woman now has a choice of dying as well, or trying to inject some life back into the relationship. She may try everything, being nice, shouting, pleading or pushing, just to get a response that contains some feeling. Eventually when all else fails and she has tried everything to shock her partner into life, she has an affair and then makes sure he finds out. Now there is a response and some life back in the relationship, for what was deeply buried in old Stonewall has been forced to the surface. Again, this is choice time for Stonewall types. Either we learn and are grateful for being woken up, or we blame our partner and hire expensive lawyers.

A note on sex addiction:

This is one of the most pervasive and powerful of all addictions because, generally, it started when we were young. As children we soon discovered that anytime we felt bad we could get relief from those feelings by some form of sex. Today, with prolific and readily available pornography on the Internet, it's easier than ever to become caught in its trap.

While there are many downsides to sex addiction, one of the worst is that of objectification. Feelings quickly become dissociated, and in order to get any feelings from the experience we need to become more and more extreme, but then the objectifying gets more entrenched and we are trapped in a vicious circle. To break this addiction we need to deal with the underlying bad feelings and get back to making love to our partner rather than using sex to hide our deeper feelings or escape the boredom in our current relationship.

✓ Try this:

If you have had an affair (or a string of them), or if you are currently resisting temptation, then the challenge is to look closely at what it is you are getting or believe you would get from such liaisons. How does this person meet your needs in the way your current partner is not? What is the quality they have that you find so attractive? That will be the key to what is missing in your relationship and what you need to have the courage to talk to your partner about. Affairs only happen when we are running away from our relationship problems. They are never a solution.

Triangles and Dilemmas

Sometimes an affair grows more serious and you might find yourself in the situation of having two partners and a dilemma about which one you really want to be with. When you are with one you start wondering what it would be like with the other and vice versa. Now you are really trapped on the horns of a dilemma. Smart as you are, you spend hours every day trying to think up a solution and even when you write down the pros and cons, you still can't make that move.

That, in fact, is the purpose of a dilemma: to set up a situation to which there is no answer – and then spend years trying to figure it out. Even if you do make a choice, there will always be part of you wondering what it would have been like if you had chosen the opposite way. So even in your choice, your mind is still divided and true love and commitment is not possible.

Of course it is tough for people who pride themselves on their brain power to be caught by a dilemma, but the answer in this situation does not come from your thinking. It comes from your understanding that you have trapped yourself. While you stay in the arms of this situation your life will not move forward. The way through is to recognise it is a trap and to have the courage to step forward in some area of your life. Then the answer to your question will appear.

Any triangular relationship reflects the basic triangle of our lives as little children with our parents. This dynamic will be with us for much of our lives and the first and most important thing is to recognise it for the trap that it is. Once we set off down the path of affairs or flings, then we will feel guilty and we will contract ourselves and withdraw our energy from our partner.

✓ Try this:

For every one of us, the next step in our life is different depending on our life path, and at different moments on that path. Your next step right now might be to value yourself, to become more equal, to speak more, to accept advice from others, to ask for help, to stop being busy, to give up an addiction, to commit to something or someone, to let something or someone go, to forgive yourself - the list is as varied and endless as people on the planet.

An affair is rarely the answer. More often it is a distraction and a way of keeping you trapped from taking your next step, which could blossom within your relationship and thereby enhance it.

Always keep your energy and thoughts inside your relationship. Keep committing even when your head tells you to run, and have the courage to turn around and face what you need to face. Communicate with honesty and keep choosing your partner, for to be in love is to want to marry every day.

Part Four:

THE NEW PARADIGM OF RELATIONSHIPS

'The salvation of man is through love and in love.'

Viktor Frankl

Back in Part One of this book, we looked at the common cultural myths we hold about relationships. One of the most insidious is the idea that once you have found Mr or Ms Right then you have arrived; all your needs will be taken care of, all your pain will melt away – and, joy of joys, you will live 'happily ever after'.

Thinking we have arrived at our final happiness destination is always a mistake. Yet this illusion pervades much of the personal and spiritual development movements. There are many people who will sell you their amazing weekend workshop or therapy process, claiming it will transform your life forever. *'Oh,'* we think, *'maybe if I just do this workshop, then I will be happy, then I will finally be sorted.'*

We don't believe life is like that. It is going to throw you curveballs from time to time; you are going to be continually challenged. Life is a journey and we are here to learn and to grow – we are here to *evolve*. And, as we have said before, one of the best and fastest (though not necessarily the easiest) ways to do that is in a relationship. And the happiest, most fulfilling relationships are those that evolve and grow, that support each partner to evolve and grow, not just slowly dissolve.

Rewriting the Love Rules

Our current paradigm of relationships does not work. We need to collectively dump this idea of 'happy ever after' and that our partner should meet our needs all of the time. True love isn't about bargaining and blame, it is about giving, for-giving and going beyond our petty ego needs.

All relationships are either getting better or getting worse. Like thoughts, relationships move in a direction, and that direction can be changed. The direction is up to us. No matter how bad things have become, if we are willing we can turn it around. As long as we are prepared to learn and change we can have the relationship that is our hearts' desire.

We're not going to give you a ten-step plan to married bliss, or an easy self-help list. What we are going to set out for you here is what we have learned over many years of trying and failing again and again, of making every mistake in the relationship book, and yet succeeding in creating a loving, lasting marriage, despite it all. There isn't a formula for a great relationship, but there are a set of principles and a toolkit that we can apply in any situation, and that we have tried and tested and that work for us. For it to work for you too, take these principles on board and practise, practise, practise. Do your own research. If these principles work then you will know: things will get better!

So let's look at what we believe to be the true purpose of relationship (Chapter 10), the principles of evolved relating (Chapter 11) and the skills you need to make your relationship work (Chapter 12). Finally, we will show you how to have a good break up, if it is time for you to move on from your current partner.

Chapter 10
THE PURPOSE OF RELATIONSHIPS

Purpose #1: Getting Past the Ego

Back in Part One, we looked at what happens to us as we grow up from tiny, innocent babies, from being 'nobodies' to becoming 'somebodies' in the world. We saw how we build up our ego structure throughout our formative years to become functioning, 'rational' adults – and in the process, we saw how that ego structure gets skewed and adapted to compensate for the pain of our unmet childhood needs.

A healthy sense of self is essential for day-to-day functioning; we need to have a good sense of who we are; know where our personal boundaries lie; what we are prepared to do for others and where we 'draw the line.' This is especially true in parenting! Anyone who has brought up young children will tell you that without firm yet fair boundaries, children will keep pushing to find out where the limits are.

The thing about the ego is that it believes in separation. When it gets out of hand – as it often does in situations like cut-throat business dealings – it gets competitive, ruthless and obsessed with its own importance. This is one reason why reality TV can be so entertaining; people enjoy watching egos collide and the drama that ensues.

It is our ego selves who fight our partner to get our needs met, to be in control and therefore not have to feel our painful buried emotions. It is our ego selves who believe in win-lose, rather than win-win in our relationship dramas. It is our ego that is confronted every time we get upset.

We spend much of our adult lives unpicking our skewed ego structure. Born a blank slate, eventually we will die and merge back into the mysterious place from whence we came. Our growth as human beings – especially once we have survived a mid life crisis – is a process of unravelling, of returning to our 'original goodness', our original innocent state. It is also about understanding the falseness of the skewed ego structure, and meeting and resolving the pain that caused it to form its unique constellation within us in the first place.

Feeling our feelings is not the most popular leisure activity. People spend their whole lives avoiding having anything to do with their emotional selves (something the British are particularly good at). We numb out with all manner of addictions, compulsive and obsessive behaviours. We would, generally, much rather zone out in front of the TV than feel our aching loneliness or address our unexpressed grief. However, once you have the courage to feel whatever comes up, you will, in time, get to experience what we call your original 'shining light', the part of you who is connected to the whole of creation. This is what we call oneness or 'big love'; and it is a blissful experience to hang out here for any length of time.

We fall in love blind to the fact that love will not save us from our pain. Quite the opposite. Love will, eventually, *bring up* all that pain, in order for it to be healed and resolved. Love will, if we allow it, dissolve the skewed competitive, separate ego self. It is our opinion and experience that true love pushes you out of your unhealthy ego structure, out of separation, and, ultimately, into partnership, oneness and the understanding that we are all but separate expressions of one unified whole.

Purpose #2: Reflecting Back Your Unhealed Self

Our ego minds are complex animals. Back in Chapter 3 we looked at how the conscious and subconscious minds work. Our conscious, rational self, is, remember, the smallest part of who we are. But in this age of science and reason, this goes largely overlooked. Much of the academic, scientific world bases itself on the concept of an impartial observer. But, is it even possible for anyone to observe anything impartially?

Most of us act as if our conscious world is solid and based on absolute truths. But if ten people witnessed an accident, would they all come up with exactly the same eye-witness report? No, the reports would differ. When siblings and parents recall family events, their accounts can differ wildly too. Who is right? Is anyone right?

We cannot see the world around us as it actually is, we can only see it through the filters of our minds. And we certainly do not see others for who they actually are. An off the cuff remark from our partner that might seem 'insensitive' or hurtful to us, can often sound perfectly reasonable to the next person. Our unique positive and negative reactions to other people give us constant clues about ourselves.

We can never fully see ourselves – we need others to reflect ourselves back to us and your partner is the perfect person to do that. The chemistry between you, if you remember, is about your subconscious iceberg selves meeting and clicking. There is no logic or rationale to it; you just feel it, you just know that you want to be with this person.

In fact, if you ever want to know what is buried in your subconscious mind (and therefore automatically driving you on a deeper level) then take a good look at your partner – they will be acting it out perfectly.

Client Story:

Jennifer was a good-looking woman in her thirties who sat for two days in one of our workshops, saying very little. Eventually she got to speak and her composure went. Breaking down in tears, she recounted how her relationship had recently collapsed. Her partner just walked out and left her.

After listening to the story, we asked her to set her conscious mind aside and answer the following question with the first response that came to her mind: 'Why did she want the relationship to end?' The reaction of other participants in the workshop was shock, for we had obviously not been listening. But Jennifer's face told a different story. It lit up with a huge smile (which often happens when a subconscious aspect is brought to light). She went on to say how she felt this relationship had been holding her back. It dawned on her that on some level she had left the relationship first. Her partner had actually reflected her own doubts perfectly.

The bulk of our actions and behaviours is powered by our subconscious drives, that vast iceberg of complex feelings and emotions that glides around with us throughout our lives, until we are willing to look at it head on. It is hard to accept that as mature, logical beings, often with high-powered jobs, PhDs or other successes under our belts, we are not the rational creatures we thought we were. It is hard to admit that we actually don't know ourselves at all.

The best way to know yourself, as we have said before, is by accepting that your partner is reflecting all those hidden subconscious complexes back to you, in the magic mirror of relationship.

✓ Try this:

Revisit our story in Our Perceptions are Projections, page 105 in Power Struggle stage.

Or try this: think of two situations you consciously believe you didn't want to happen in your present relationship, or in your last relationship. Now ask yourself, in relation to each situation, the intuitive question, *'If I were to know, why did I want this situation? What did it allow me to do or say? How did it suit me somehow?'*

Trust the first answer that pops into your mind, however unexpected it may seem.

Purpose #3: Learning to Give and Receive Love

The Vietnamese Buddhist teacher Thich Nhat Hanh once said:

When you plant lettuce, if it does not grow well, you don't blame the lettuce. You look for reasons it is not doing well. It may need fertiliser, or more water, or less sun. You never blame the lettuce. Yet if we have problems with our friends or family, we blame the other person. But if we know how to take care of them, they will grow well, like the lettuce. Blaming has no positive effect at all, nor does trying to persuade using reason and argument. That is my experience. No blame, no reasoning, no argument, just understanding. If you understand, and you show that you understand, you can love, and the situation will change.

We treat plants with thoughtful kindness and loving support, why not our partners? Why not our families? No one around us is going to get any better unless we give him or her our love and understanding; the world out there is only going to shift, if we are willing to shift. Only by changing ourselves will we make a difference. That is the power of love; it changes everything – and the place we learn that is in our relationships. If love is what makes the difference, then when you become bored of your partner, when you know their habits, likes, dislikes and sexual preferences, is the answer to change them? If we go down this path we will hit that bored point sooner and sooner – and our relationships will have shorter and shorter time spans. Over the years we have heard thousands of people complain about their partner's shortcomings. But after some self-examination, they discover the thing they are complaining about is what they are also doing to some degree.

It is essential that we use our partner as our barometer, our own personal reflection of what we are secretly doing. When they are happy and doing well it is because we have been giving and the reverse is also true: If your partner has a problem then you have a problem – and at the core of every problem, there is something we are not giving.

OUR STORY: Learning to Give

Sue says:

In our relationship, an area of friction was around handling money, paying bills and keeping records.

> After we got back together again I felt it was Jeff's turn to take care of our finances. He agreed as he was eager to please me, but within six months we were in all kinds of trouble: the phone was cut off, there were red electricity bills, no cheque stubs had been filled out and we were overdrawn.
>
> Part of me wanted to gloat that he was so irresponsible, but then I realised that I could give this practical help to our relationship. For me it was no big deal. I obviously found it easier than Jeff to manage our finances, so why wouldn't I just do it? As I did so, I saw there were lots of other ways Jeff gave to our relationship and I could appreciate them better. It also changed how we discussed money. Instead of being an area to be avoided, there was more teamwork. Because the truth is Jeff can make (as well as spend) money easily, and since we have combined our talents, there has been much more abundance and success.

As we give truly in our relationship, things will change and move forward. If you believe you are giving and nothing changes then that is sacrifice; giving with an agenda, is not true giving.

If you ever notice a 'significant other' around you – especially your life partner – failing in any way, then it means you have stopped giving and started taking from them. Either that or you are competing with them. The answer is to give up our judgments on them and instead extend ourselves to them, reach out to love and support them. As we give what we have in the relationship, they will give back to an equal extent – they will bloom and change before our eyes.

All of us want a great partner and we may spend hours fantasising about one; if only we did then how happy we would be, living the romantic dream life that is the stuff of our great love songs. But if you *really* want a great partner, then you have to become that great partner. It is a two way street.

✓ Try this:

Make a list of everything you want in a partner. Take your time and be thorough; what are all the attributes that would contribute to this being a successful and long-lasting relationship?

Once you have enthusiastically compiled your list, ask yourself, 'Am I those things? Am I willing to become those things so I can be a 100% partner?'

It is through our true, unconditional giving that we learn the next great lesson of life: the art of receiving – because what we give always comes back to us. Learning how to give and receive in equal amounts is the greatest lesson of relationships and partnerships. It sets up a flow in our lives, it moves us forward and creates abundance. The highs become higher and the lows are never quite as low again.

Purpose #4: Happiness and Success

Happiness and success in life is a common purpose for all of us. If we are not happy, there is a second common purpose: to heal ourselves until we reach happiness again.

Our happiness comes from learning to have great relationships, with our partner, our friends, our children and, of course, the trickiest place of all, within our birth family. The most obvious place to start however, is with your significant other, because everything that is broken in our minds will come up within a committed relationship. We then have a choice; either blame the other person, demand that they change, get rid of them, or... Or we take responsibility for our feelings, communicate honestly about them, resolve the issue and move on – for within every problem there is a gift, a lesson, an insight, if you look at it from the right perspective. There is always something to learn about ourselves.

This process is how relationships evolve – and it is how you evolve too. You get to move past your psychology, your skewed ego structure, past your old limiting subconscious beliefs to a more successful and abundant life. Working through your patterns together (or alone – it only takes one, remember), means you get to have more honeymoons as you spiral back into a new level of harmony, communication and understanding with each other. Issues, it seems, often come round in spirals; we go through them layer after layer. Time and again, our clients tell us that once they have worked through a layer of issues with their partner, their lives open up, things start to flow and there is more success and happiness in their lives. They reach partnership and true intimacy.

The keys to the door of happiness are presented in the next chapter, eight principles distilled from all the advice and examples in Parts 1 – 3 of this book. Where relevant, we have cross-referenced these principles with exercises that make them real and give you the tools to keep that promise of lasting love alive.

Chapter 11

EIGHT PRINCIPLES OF EVOLVED RELATING

Principle #1: Your Happiness is Your Own Responsibility

Many of us spend our days jumping around different places in our minds, looking for what it is that will make us happy. One of the greatest expectations we lay on our partner, or potential partner, is that it is their job to make us happy. But when we really examine this belief it does not take long to realise how insane it is.

Take a good look at your partner and ask yourself, does this person have what it takes to make you happy? Do they have a PhD in happiness? Most likely not; most likely they are looking at you to provide exactly the same thing. Many of us made this same demand from our parents. We thought that it was their duty to make us happy. Again, how capable were they of that task?

Do you want a perfectly miserable partner who believes it is your job to make them happy? Then why expect someone else to do the same for you? If you are not happy in your life then there is something that needs looking at, something to be changed. Only you can confront, shift and heal the bad feelings that drag you down. Of course, it is great if you can do that within a relationship – but the responsibility for your own happiness lies with you alone.

Principle #2: Your Needs are Your Own Responsibility

We see our partner or spouse or even our children as being placed on this planet in order to fulfill our needs.

But our needs are like this hole in us that was created way back in childhood when we judged our parents or carers, complaining that, in one way or another, they did not take care of us.

In any upset, any fight, we are saying that our partner is not taking care of our needs. We become indignant about this. It is outrageous! How dare they not meet our needs?! Angry, we resort to emotional blackmail. We force them to meet our needs by laying a guilt trip on them.

When we become really needy and then try and take from others around us we become draining; we become 'sucks' or 'energy vampires.' Children have radar for such people. When the needy aunt or uncle comes to visit, you notice that within a few minutes the kids have all left the room.

Client Story:

Years ago a woman regularly attended our workshops and on several occasions we talked to her about her overtly needy energy. But often people caught in such a place are unaware of how their behaviour affects others. Her husband worked overseas, a lot, and her three sons volunteered for boarding school and left home as soon as possible. Our son, a healthy teenager, sat next to her for a session in a workshop and afterwards told us the whole of his left side, the side next to her, was numb. She had sucked all his energy out and he couldn't bear to sit close to her again. Later, she told us that she could finally see what she had been doing and then quickly set about repairing the damage.

When we manipulate someone, we are conniving to have our needs met. It might work in the short term, but over time it will pollute the space around us and others will instinctively back off. This is the acid test in any relationship; if anyone moves away from you at any time for any reason, it is because you are trying to take from them in some way – you are trying to get them to meet your needs.

Another common strategy is to pretend we don't have any needs. 'I don't need anyone or anything!' is the cry of our independence. We have seen countless independent people arrive at a place where they have nobody – and then fall to pieces.

Jeff says:

This was my favourite strategy for almost forty years. I was totally independent and would metaphorically shoot needy people on sight. I believed I needed nobody, and nobody was going to tell me what to do. As far as I was concerned, I did not have a needy bone in my body, not a needy gene in my being. Asking for help was never an option.

When I realised that acting like this had driven everyone away, even my children, I fell into the chasm of aching neediness, the place which I had sworn was not in me. When I really felt the pain of my unmet needs, I understood why I had resisted it for so long, why I had sworn on a stack of bibles that this neediness was not in me. It took me many months of the worst feelings for me to climb back into my life.

It is important here that we don't give needs a bad rap. It is perfectly normal and natural to have needs. The problem arises when we try and get others to take care of them. Naturally, if you care for your partner and they have a need why would you not give to them? You could recognise it is your choice. It is great when your partner gives to you in a way that fills that hole inside of you. But it is essential we stay in integrity about our needs and acknowledge them, rather than run or hide from them. Do whatever you can to take care of your own needs first and foremost.

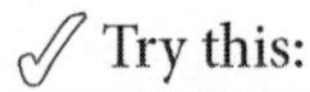

The Best Way to Get What You Need is to Give it

Think about it. If you know you need something, then you know something is missing within you. The reason we can see something is missing is because we already have that very quality inside of us. Deep down, it is actually our true nature. It just so happens that it got covered over with a frozen pocket of pain of unmet childhood needs. Yes, this is painful – and painful feelings are part of the deal of being human.

However, our challenge here is firstly, to lay off blaming our partner for our unmet needs, and secondly to stop wallowing in the *'if only my parents loved me properly, I would have a better life'* scenario.

If you are a parent (and if you aren't you can imagine for a moment that you are), then imagine that your child wants something, say food, warmth, love, attention or a cuddle. If you have that resource to give, then do you give it? Of course you do and to the best of your ability. If this is the case, then were your parents really any different? No. In fact your parents gave you everything they had.

Now, can you see that maybe it is your calling to give this gift, this quality you have, both to yourself and to your parents? The best way to get what we need is to give it – because what you give is what you get.

Principle #3: Your Feelings are Your Own Responsibility

Let's go back to the iceberg model again on page 34 and have a look at where our feelings come from. That's right, from you! From the mass of subconscious beliefs and emotions that you carry with you throughout life. Certain situations like war and atrocity will make you feel sad and angry, which is a normal and appropriate response. But when it comes to relationships, it is important to realise that your feelings are actually a choice. This choice usually happens within a subconscious split second – you have to be very aware to even catch it. But it is still a choice.

Naturally, our first reaction to these statements is disbelief. '*Noooo!*' we scream inwardly. '*This cannot be true! Last week when my partner forgot our anniversary, he made me feel totally unloved and abandoned.*'

Let's take a minute and look carefully at this idea. Our reaction to our perception of being '*unloved and abandoned*' is our reaction; someone else in the same situation might not be bothered by the situation at all – a bit miffed maybe, but not totally unloved and abandoned.

The chances are that this feeling was inside us long before we ever met our partner who triggers it in us now. Most of us repress our feelings; we may have been taught they are a sign of weakness or at least that they cause trouble. As we work hard to stifle and push down those feelings, we become walking time bombs; like one of those Second World War sea mines bobbing around in the ocean until someone comes too close and then: 'Boom!' Watch out! While we are young and have plenty of energy we can keep this mess of feelings buried. But as we get older, we run out of energy and patience; we become more irritable and volatile.

✓ Try this:

When something or someone pushes a button and triggers your repressed negative feelings, resist the temptation to either blame and attack or withdraw. Recognise that these feelings are yours and have probably been yours for a long time. You could even get to the point of welcoming the person or situation that has given you the opportunity to get hold of old negative feelings that you otherwise manage to push down or dissociate from.

Now, heal the old feelings. Pull out the iceberg model and go to work.

Principle #4: You are Never Upset for the Reasons You Think You Are

When our partner acts in a certain way (you know, that way that really drives you nuts) or speaks with that incredibly irritating tone of voice, and we have a strong negative emotional reaction, we assume our feelings are all about what is happening now. We insist on sticking to that stance, even when, time after time, people in our lives appear to act in exactly the same way – and we continue to respond in exactly the same way. This is a pattern, and we are caught in a loop. We are condemned to repeat the pattern until we either totally shut down and don't let anyone close (and even then you will still repeat the pattern with your friends, work colleagues or neighbours); or we recognise our response for what it is, take responsibility and start to change at a much deeper level.

Try this:

When we are upset very little of what is going on is about now. The rest is about something that happened long, long ago. Have a think for a minute. What is the thing your partner does that really winds you up, that you really hate? Enter the feeling of it, notice what it does to you, how it feels in your body. For example, it might feel like... Or could be experienced like... Spend a few minutes really paying attention, almost as if you were an emotional x-ray machine looking at how your body responds to the emotion. Now, is this really the very first time you have felt that way? When did it all begin? Who are you really mad at?

Sit and if you like, take out a journal and write out the answers to those questions. What did you learn? How would you like to respond instead?

One of our clients, for example, discovered that the reason he couldn't trust his partner was because his mother had suddenly left him alone at age four.

> He hadn't heard her explain she had to look after an emergency because he was engrossed in play. When he found her gone he panicked and that fear of unexpected abandonment was still inside him. When he released the emotional memory by allowing himself to feel it and let it go, he felt free of the fear in the present.

At the heart of every upset is a misunderstanding. We need to go to the root of the issue and do our healing and transformation there, instead of holding our partner and our family hostage to our past. We make our loved ones pay now for our past mistakes, when we were just beginning to wire our brains and making those early choices that created our belief systems. We are doomed to repeat our patterns until we have the courage and integrity to deal with them.

Principle #5: Control Does Not Work

Most of us have been to the Olympics in control and the reason for that is we went to the children's Olympics in heartbreak. If you believe you missed that event in your childhood then take a look at your present and past relationships. Do you notice a trail of heartbreaks? Well, guess what? They are yours!

Our strategy to ensure we never ever suffer any future heartbreak is to try and control other people and situations. It is understandable. We want to make our world safe; we don't want to face our negative emotions. But the truth is, control doesn't work. Sooner or later it will lead us back to the very emotion we were trying to avoid in the first place.

Our control leads us into fights as we saw from the power struggle stage of relationships. In our fights we may use anger to try and change our partners and their actions. This policy is doomed to failure. Well, you might not consider it failure but we are faced with a simple choice here: do we want happiness or control? Do we want love or control? These are two opposite energies and they can't co-exist. We do need to choose.

Over the years we have spoken to thousands of people who are not in a relationship. Consciously they yearn for a relationship and go through all sorts of dating agencies to find one. While they meet lots of people, none of the relationships seems to go very far. One of the principle dynamics going on here is that we won't allow ourselves to fall in love – because we would then have to surrender and give up our control. Yet, that is the essence of falling in love: your life expands tenfold, your world is filled with endless possibilities, your mind opens up and anything could happen. Twice in one night if you are lucky!

Control is the opposite of trust. When we control others we are saying, *'I don't trust myself to handle the feelings that are coming up.'* When we control we lose trust in ourselves and our abilities and therefore we lose confidence in ourselves and in the people around us.

You can't be in control and in love. Remember when you were madly in love? When you could hardly focus on anything, could hardly cross the street, hardly get dressed you were so giddy? You could get undressed no problem at all but when you are in love, the one thing you are not is in control.

Principle #6: You Cannot Change Anyone – Except Yourself

Another way our control manifests itself is by trying to change our partner. If only they were more this way or that way, if they were more loving, more attentive, we say to ourselves, *then* we would be happy.

As we have seen though, controlling others does not work. Real, personal change always comes from an inner impulse rather than a set of external imposed rules or demands. Do you enjoy being dictated to? Being told how to be? Your partner might comply to your rules about how they should behave, but will secretly harbour resentment towards you.

The self-help guru Dr Wayne Dyer once said: '*When you change the way you look at things, the things you look at change.*' The strange thing is that when you change, usually your partner does too.

Principle #7: All Relationships Are in Perfect Balance

Every relationship balances out somehow, and in that balancing there is always a level of collusion at a deeper level. Naturally there are positions we fight for, like being the independent one, so your partner has to take the emotionally dependent position. Equally, people will fight to be the 'good' one in the marital breakup.

It is common for us to hear in our workshops about how a certain partner was wronged and that they have come to the workshop for some answers. They are then often astounded when one of our first questions is: '*Why did you want this to happen?*' Their first response is nearly always: '*This was the last thing I wanted!*' But as we have said, that is to only play to the conscious mind, the smallest part of ourselves. If you want to truly understand yourself, recognise that if something happened with your partner, then, at some level, it was because that was also your plan.

Sue says:

On the surface I swore our break-up was the last thing I wished to happen. But when I was willing to ask myself the deeper question: *'Why did I want to break up with Jeff?'* the answer that swam up from my subconscious was: *'Because it's too much hassle, because I want to do things my way without all this pain.'* It astonished me that underneath all the 'poor me' victim stance, was actually a similar level of independence as Jeff was expressing. That part of me had wanted out just as much as he did.

Part of the attraction between two people in the honeymoon stage is that all our broken pieces and all their broken pieces fit together perfectly. If you have a painful story about how someone in your childhood betrayed you and broke your heart, they too will have a very similar story. Of course, this isn't obvious at first, but at some later stage in the relationship it will surface. If there is no awareness of it, one partner will end up doing the betraying and the other will feel totally betrayed. The reason this happens in the present is not to punish us for our past. It is to give us an opportunity to resolve whatever set the pattern up in the first place. Of course it hurts, but it is what is needed to be resolved in order for us to move on in life – to move towards true happiness.

If this isn't recognised, it is easy for the relationship to polarise into a good guy, bad guy scenario. In some relationships the fights over the polarisation are so great, the relationship is short lived. Even so, we have found couples who have polarised and then spent twenty years or more living the life of the living dead because they haven't looked at the underlying wound that is begging to be healed.

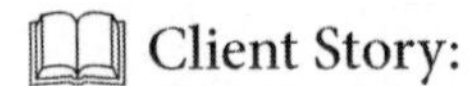

In one of our workshops in Germany, a woman in a thirty-year marriage embedded in the dead zone said she wanted to find the courage to finally leave her partner. They had assumed opposite roles: he was Mr. Couch Potato and she was Mrs. Capable, taking care of everything. But when she understood her part in the situation, and found her own fear of the relationship moving towards more intimacy, she realised how she had polarised with her partner. She went home and within a few hours she was back at the honeymoon stage with her husband, where they then proceeded to make up for lost time.

If you find yourself saying things about your partner like: *'I would never be that angry!'* or *'I would never behave in that way,'* then you are beginning to polarise. What we see in our partner is also in us; we have the good bits and the bad bits of both. When we both examined our relationship, we realised our partner had never done anything to us that we had not done to them, or to someone else.

If we can admit: Sure I can be kind but also I can be cruel, I can be loving but I also have parts that are angry or even violent, then we can be more honest and authentic. If we deny this, then someone around us will, invariably, act it out.

 Client Story:

One of our workshop participants told us about a friend of hers who ran 'Connect to Your Angel' workshops. She was, by all accounts, a very sweet person, filled with light and purity – but her partner used to attack her verbally in public. In fact, in one of her workshops, her husband openly questioned her and responded to her replies with such terminology as: 'Bollocks!'

As she was so kind and forgiving, she 'let it go' but in the next weekend workshop he did the same, this time with more aggression. Back in the hotel room, he slapped her. She was in such a state she cancelled the rest of the workshop and proceeded to tell the world how awful her husband was. Well, it is true there is rarely a good reason to hit anyone but when she moved into super good, sweet pretence he had nowhere to go but to balance her off. So he became the partner from hell. It is easy to see how 'off' he was in his behaviour, but she did not get how 'off' she was in hers. He was acting out her shadow self perfectly.

Try this:

This story illustrates two extremes. But is there an echo here for you? Are you taking on more of the 'good, saintly role' or the 'bad, aggressive role' in your relationship? If you are aware of this dynamic, take time to centre yourself by feeling into the core of your being. When you bring yourself back to centre then the relationship rebalances.

Principle #8: Relationships Are 100%-100% Deal

This is one of the principles that we often get the strongest reactions to. For most people in our blame and compensation culture, even saying their relationship is 50%-50% deal is an enormous stretch. 'But 100%-100%?' they ask. 'You're kidding, right?'

When people insist on their relationship being a 50%-50% deal, then it gives them permission to blame their partner for something that is not working between them. As you can imagine, we have heard many people complain about their partners: they don't want sex anymore, they are withdrawn, they are aggressive and so on. But when we look closely it is soon clear that all these judgments hide the complaining partner's hidden dysfunctions: fear of sex, fear of intimacy and their hidden aggression.

When we attack or blame our partner for anything, we are really just attacking ourselves. They reflect us, remember? In fact, we will stay stuck with the problem until we are willing to take more responsibility for ourselves *and* for our partner and their behaviours.

Of course your partner has their issues – we are not saying they are as pure as the driven snow. Neither of you is 100% to blame for what happens between you. What we are saying is that you are 100% responsible for your life – you have the ability to respond appropriately, to ask yourself: *'If my partner is a reflection of my subconscious, then what does this say about me? What do I need to learn here? Why would I want it this way?'*

Haven't you noticed how you or friends of yours tend to attract the same kind of partner? Don't you or they go through the same kinds of issues in relationships? So, no matter how terrible you believe your partner's behaviour to be, why would you want it this way? Isn't there something for you to learn here?

In fact, we say that giving anything less than 100% in your relationship is a failing grade! Giving 130% will set you on the path to happiness. Taking total responsibility for yourself, your world and the people in it is how you become truly empowered. You will have no greater opportunity to do this than within a committed relationship.

Chapter 12

THE EVOLVED RELATIONSHIP TOOLKIT

Have the Courage to Be Wrong

Do you want to be right or do you want to be happy?

After all the years we have both been working on ourselves, learning transformational principles like projection and transference, we can still fall for this one. We often catch ourselves thinking: *'I do know about projection and I do know about not trying to change others. In most cases it works but in this situation, that person really is the south end of a north-going camel! About this one, I am right. That is the way this person is, and so I am justified in behaving towards them in the way that I am.'*

It might be true that you are right about part of what is going on but you are not right about the whole picture. You might even be right about the way you see it – but that is only the way you see it. In order not to get caught in a fight, you need to have the whole of your partner's energy in the solution, which will take you forward in your relationship. However, if you insist on being right, your partner will be as right as you but in the opposite direction. Now you have a fight on your hands and no-one truly wins a fight, especially if it is with your partner.

To avoid conflicts in our lives and in our relationships, we learn to build bridges and include others and their views in our thinking. Even on those *very* rare occasions when you are actually right, you still need to include your partner in the outcome because you need their energy to be successful at the next level of your relationship and your life.

Let Go of Judgment and Blame

When we judge someone, we are stuck with that person in that situation being that way we judge it to be, until we discover, once again to our horror, that actually we are not right. Consider this: if we insist on being right about someone, that they really are the way we judge them to be, then every time we see them or think of them we feel the same upset. We continue silently (or not so silently) to complain about them and the way they are. As they are usually a significant person in our life, no doubt we think of them often. It is us who is then unhappy and ill at ease. It is us, the one who judges, who loses sleep.

Our judgment freeze-frames our world. When we are being right about the way the world is, sooner or later we will start feeling stuck: stuck in our relationship, stuck in our career or stuck in life.

Jeff says:

Some ancient indigenous cultures cannot understand the Western blame culture. I remember hearing a story about Malidoma Some, the Western educated author from the Dagara Tribe of West Africa. When he attempted to explain the Western concept of suing others for compensation to his village elders, they looked puzzled. After some time, one of them asked: *'How then, do these people ever learn anything?'*

Blaming someone stops any resolution and progress. It sows resentment and if we start to make an art form out of blaming, we then become righteous, which is so unattractive. Have you ever been at the receiving end of a righteous outburst? Do you remember how bad you felt? Well that is how bad *they* feel under all that righteousness. The extent of a person's righteousness is also the extent of how wrong and bad they subconsciously feel about themselves. The extent to which they are not forgiving and tolerant with others is also the extent to which they are not forgiving and tolerant of themselves – and what they believe they have done in their past.

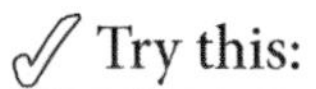

Try this:

Think of something your partner does that upsets you. Now ask yourself: *'Is this the first time this has happened? Is this the first significant person in my life who has acted this way?'* Dwell on this for a while and then ask: *'Have I ever acted this way?'* If the answer is yes, recognise how you have judged yourself in the same way you are now judging your partner. What is called for here is a little forgiveness. For as you forgive another, you forgive yourself.

Client Story:

We were teaching this principle in a workshop when a woman had a strong reaction. She claimed that her father was a dogmatic, overbearing monster and she would never ever be like that. She added that she was the one attending the workshop, working on her self-development, so how dare I suggest that she was behaving in that manner? It was true she had created this style of appearing super tolerant while having this blame towards her father of being super intolerant. I explained to her that underneath her father's behaviour he was being right. Then I explained to her that she was also being right about the way her father was. She was blaming him for what she was doing. She was making him wrong, just as he had been making her wrong.

It took emotional courage and the support of the group, but in the moment that she accepted that she and her father were being equally dogmatic, she forgave him and also herself, and her life moved forward. She told us that the next time she saw her father, things were much lighter between them and she could even joke with him about his strong opinions.

This is not about condoning bad behaviour. Rather it is about taking full responsibility for one's own behaviour. Remember, you cannot change anyone except yourself. Staying stuck in blame, although easy and obvious, doesn't help anyone, least of all yourself.

Know that Anger Is a Cover Up

Anger is a cover emotion. If someone behaves in a certain way around us it triggers an emotion – but instead of dealing with this emotion, we get angry. In our anger we attack the person we believe is responsible for triggering it. We are using our anger to control, to force people around us to act in a certain way in order that we don't feel our bad feelings. Yet, most likely, that feeling was inside us long before we met the intended target of our anger. We use our anger as a form of emotional blackmail.

Jeff says:

One of the things that made me angry in my Psychology of Vision training was being told there was never ever a good reason to be angry. How could that be true? I was outraged! But after years of work in this field I now understand that when we become angry, we are making it all about us and our defence. The person we are angry with could just as well be an object; we could place a paper bag over their head and we would still be just as angry. We have totally disconnected from those around us and we feel it is OK to rant. We want to make someone else feel guilty for what we're experiencing. We have given up our power and responsibility and now think it is OK to inflict misery on others because of our unwillingness to face an emotion, to deal with a feeling. When anger comes up for me now, I give myself a personal time limit of five minutes – any more and I know I am being righteous.

Now let's be real and recognise that we all get angry from time to time. It's normal. Anger should never be denied or repressed. It simply has to be felt.

As children, many of us were taught that it was not OK to be angry. What an enlightened parent would have said was: *'It is not a problem that you are angry, it is just not OK to burn down the garage or beat up your younger brother or sister.'*

Anger causes mayhem whether projected outward or inward towards oneself. We might even go for years never being angry until one day some little thing triggers us and we erupt. Of course, we then do something we regret – and in our guilt, then make the decision to never ever be angry again. But then we have to live life as if we are walking on eggshells. We live in constant fear that if we are not super careful, the monster that is our anger will come out at the most inappropriate time and drive a huge truck through our life.

✓ Try this:

Accept your anger. When you get angry, recognise it. Don't act on it and don't run away from it. Let it burn inside you and move through and out of you. Then see what feelings come up. What is the deeper emotion that your anger has been defending against? What is it telling you? The simple act of accepting the fact we are angry allows us to reintegrate that aspect of us and just not let it be a big deal. As we accept and integrate our anger, it becomes something else; a force for change, passion for life, the fuel that drives our creativity.

When we become angry for a long time, we are stuck in the belief that someone or something is depriving us of something. It might look as if someone has 'done us wrong' and deprived us of achieving a certain goal or state but, in truth, no one can deprive us except ourselves. We are the captain of our ship, the master of our fate; we could learn to refocus, learn to adapt and find a better way.

It is not OK in a relationship to get angry and stay angry, or to use your anger as a weapon against anyone else. Nobody comes out unscarred when we are angry, for anger is like a machine gun. It gets everybody including ourselves.

Stay With the 'What Is'

The first step in transforming our difficult emotions is to take responsibility for them – because they are ours. We call this process staying with the 'What Is...', a model that we teach in our workshops.

It starts with a triggering event, for example when our partner does or says something that riles us. Within an instant, our subconscious feelings erupt and we have a reaction, an emotional response, such as furious rage or deep sadness.

In this moment we can choose to stop and stay with those feelings – a difficult task at the best of times, we know. The thing about feelings though, is that they just want to be felt. But we have become masters at avoiding doing so, usually because at the time we first experienced them as children, they were so overwhelming it felt like we might die.

Rather than feel terrible, we tend to choose to go into some kind of activity to avoid the pain – we might become workaholics, disappear off to the pub, splurge on credit cards or devour a couple of packets of chocolate biscuits in one go. We call this a failure of intelligence. This compensatory behaviour becomes compulsive; it is what fuels all kinds of addictions and disorders. It sends us into panic, anxiety and dissociation. Most importantly, this compensatory behaviour masks the pain, which means we will only be triggered again at some future moment.

The Buddha has been quoted as saying:

> *All happiness comes from the desire for others to be happy.*
> *All misery comes from the desire for oneself to be happy.*

Your suffering actually comes from your unwillingness to suffer. Pain is part of the deal of being human but the good news is that when you open your heart to your pain, when you allow it to simply be there, it *will* eventually dissipate. This is not to say you should take no action at all. Sometimes a burst of anger is a great way to get the housework done. The trick is to be aware; again, don't run from it, but don't react to it either. See what it has got to tell you, because there is a lesson in there for you somewhere. Feeling your feelings will take you to your heart – and only when you are calmly centred in your heart, can you respond to any situation intelligently.

Our pain always comes from a misunderstanding. It was not that our parents did not love and care for us; they did. They just did not love and care for themselves. It has become clear over 20 years of teaching about relationships that everyone in every situation is doing the best they can, given their inner and outer circumstances, given their past. Sure they could do better, but then so could we.

Jeff says:

> Often I will sit with an issue for days trying to see the misunderstanding. Each time I get it, I understand the other person and why they are doing what they are doing. With that understanding comes connection and love, for

> when we fully understand our partner and all that is going for them in their inner world, when we see the challenges they have had to face just to stay alive, when we see their willingness to share their lives with us and all our baggage, we can open our hearts to them. With the understanding comes gratitude. And this is the most important ingredient in our lives, because gratitude is the mother of all feelings and essential to a happy relationship.

Listen to Your Heart

This is a place of great divide for us humans: do we go with our heart or our head? When we are independent (and dissociated from our feelings) we live in our heads, at that rational logical level. In fact if we spend too much time there we become a talking head. This is understandable in today's society, where thinking has become more important than feeling, where having emotions is seen as some kind of weakness. But staying in your head means you will soon get bored with life. Maybe you earn enough money to buy excitement by doing adventurous things on weekends, but that is really just a plaster on a deep wound.

Without our hearts we are lost. We lack direction and meaning in our lives. When we live in our heads we have made the decision not to let anything have too much meaning for us – because if we do and then something goes wrong, we most likely will have to feel something. Taken to extremes we become cynics. Cynics don't want anything to mean too much so they trash everything, reduce it to having no importance so it cannot hurt them. They conduct their relationships at a superficial thinking level and keep their hearts well defended. The opposite of being a cynic is to be sincere, to be heartfelt, so that when we do fall in love and have a relationship, we let our partner matter to us. After all, love is from the heart and not from the head.

Let us learn not to fear our hearts, and to have the courage to stand up for what we really want and believe in. Many of us had those dreams about what kind of life we wanted, what kind of world we wanted, but when we gave up on our hearts we gave up on those dreams – and then we lost our way, we lost our passion and creativity. In truth, we stopped caring. We could, however, win it all back because it has not gone anywhere. It is still inside us just waiting for that ounce of courage. Without our hearts in a relationship, we are only ticking boxes. We will never truly know love and the fullest meaning of its essence.

To be successful in this life and also in our relationships we need to win back our hearts. Our hearts show us what is important. Once we know that, then our minds will help us achieve it. When both parts of us line up, we are congruent and we will be successful. In fact, we will be unstoppable.

Communicate What You Are Really Thinking

We are often asked in workshops: '*What is the quickest way out of the dead zone in a relationship?*' The answer is very simple: communicate to your partner what you are thinking about them. What creates distance in any relationship is our lack of congruence. If what we say and what we think start becoming very different things, a distance will grow in our relationships and then all sorts of things or people can come between us. Or it just becomes plain dead.

If you say what you are thinking, the one thing your relationship will not be is boring! Many people's response to this suggestion is that if they told their partner what they were thinking, it would mark the end of the relationship. Well, if you don't do it, then sooner or later the divide and deadness will grow until the relationship dies a miserable death anyway.

Go For Resolution, Not Compromise

When we compromise, one side does not get what they want. It means we have not got past the issue. In fact, the issue will continue to fester and resurface at some time in the future. It is important to take the time necessary to reach resolution, where each partner gets what he or she wants. This is the power of communication and emotional maturity – that we can have relationships and not feel like we have to lose something. Often people say that they have tried this approach but they have not been able to reach resolution, even after hours of debate. That usually means there are some hidden agendas that have not been put on the table, which makes resolution almost impossible. So this is a time for more honesty from both partners.

When we become good at communication, usually the gift of the feminine partner in most relationships, then we can begin to understand each other and express our needs and wishes with clarity. Let's face it: what do most men know about communication? Most men know as much about communication as they do about foreplay, another great act of communication.

If men are wise they will allow their woman to take the lead when it comes to addressing issues in the partnership.

Women need to learn that a man's first thought when she says: 'Darling, we need to talk', is that they will be made wrong. They remember an urgent business call or a darts match at the local pub. If the man does stay, then he generally has that look of someone in front of a firing squad. Also, women need to have the awareness that when her partner does open up, it is really not the best time to bring out her long list of grievances and start making it all about herself. There might well be a backlog of things that need to be spoken about. But if the woman becomes indulgent then the man will clam up and the opportunity will be missed.

Give up Secrets

Usually, whilst talking to someone about their relationship, the classic phrase comes up: 'Oh, but I could never tell them about *that*!'

Secrets harm relationships. We bury our secrets, our shameful actions, the parts of ourselves or our lives we are too scared to reveal to our partner, and then act as if we have never done such a thing. We can even get indignant about it, harshly judging others who have done something similar. Sometimes we get so good at burying stuff we don't like about ourselves that we go into denial; we can totally convince ourselves that we would never do – and have never, ever done – such a thing.

Every one of us has done goofy things in our lives. Every one of us has made mistakes. But if we keep them secret we do not learn – and then that becomes a place where no one else is allowed to go. In a relationship every secret will create a distance between you and your partner – and that distance will then create deadness. If you are sitting on a secret or two, a part of you shuts down to both your partner and to your life, because you are always terrified the secret will come out.

If you want a close and loving relationship, at some point you will need to tell your secrets. Honesty and integrity are essential to a working relationship. Even if you have had an affair, sooner or later you will have to speak about it. People often say to us: 'Yes, but if I told them about *that*, it would spell the end of the relationship.' But then the secret becomes like a cancer gnawing away at the loving bond you are trying to save. Not only will it cause deadness, the guilt you carry will, eventually, most likely turn into aggression – and damage the relationship further.

OUR STORY: Telling Our Secrets

Sue says:

> After Jeff and I got back together, an old secret of mine started gnawing away at me. Jeff is very intuitive, and every once in a while he would insist there was something I was keeping from him. The truth is that, very early on in our relationship, before we married or had children, I'd had a fling with a work colleague. It was secret then because he had a partner too, and I see now that my guilt was catching up with me. It got more and more tortuous and obvious to me that this secret was creating a distance between Jeff and me, so I eventually plucked up the courage to tell him – and the relief was

> immediate. Although Jeff was shocked, he forgave me. But more importantly, I was able to let go of my own shame and forgive myself. It made me so much more open and human – and busted my 'holier than thou' attitude I still had around Jeff's old pattern of having affairs.

If we learn to communicate and trust it is truly amazing what we can work through. After twenty years of helping people, of hearing a thousand relationship stories, it is our conclusion that a relationship can survive anything. As our teacher Chuck Spezzano says: 'No issues are love-proof.' Any relationship can be turned around from a total nightmare, to the most loving, caring and passionate intimacy.

Have Good Arguments

Look, unless you have one of those perfect 'never a cross word' type relationships (yeah, right), then you are going to argue. You are going to have areas of conflict to be resolved, which is, presumably, why many of you are reading this book.

We often advise partners to book an appointment with each other for at least an hour, so they can communicate honestly with each other. The following pointers are principles (not laws) to help you reach resolution. Work with them as best you can:

1. Before you start, consciously choose what kind of outcome you want from your communication.

2. To the best of your ability avoid using 'you' statements. Mostly using 'you' indicates blame, and blame stops communication. As soon as blame starts then communication has ended and

the fight or resentment is only a matter of time. Use 'I' statements instead. No-fault communication is most effective.

3. Trust the other person with what is really on your mind and be honest. Say what is really going on for you. Most likely they already know! Any 'withhold' (a thought you keep hidden) doesn't allow for resolution and actually is a form of attack that will create distance.

4. Interruption stops communication and is best avoided. We interrupt because we can't stand the feeling the communication is triggering inside us, or because the competition is too great.

5. Understand that overwhelm happens when the feelings being triggered get too much. We become overwhelming so as not to feel overwhelmed! Within a fight both partners are actually feeling the *same emotion*. The power struggle is just this ball of pain being passed back and forth.

6. Expressing appreciation ends fights, because it makes the other person more important than the pain.

7. Reach resolution by the end of your exchange. Don't compromise or impose as both will result in future problems. If people have hidden agendas then resolution will take a long time so be willing to put all your judgements and wishes on the table. Keep making those appointments. It will take as long as it takes.

Forgive Both of You

As soon as we give up being right, there is a possibility that change might start to happen. Giving up being right is the first step to freeing the situation, freeing the people around us and therefore freeing ourselves. We also need to recognise no-one around us will change until we give to them, that we give forth to them, that we for-give. It is our forgiveness that will change everything.

Many times in workshops people have talked about feeling rejected by their parents, and the difficulty they have forming relationships through fear of further rejection. When we work through this dynamic, people can see that they also rejected their parent, or ex-partners, or whoever they felt rejected them. What they saw as rejection could have been interpreted in a different way: the parent might have felt overwhelmed or upset; the partner may have had the same rejection issue but jumped ship first. What becomes clear is that the rejected one slammed the door on forgiveness and understanding. When they understand and forgive the other person, then they also understand and forgive themselves.

During workshops we often hear people speak about how one parent or the other took off and left them, presumably out of self-interest or lack of care and love. However, if we take a participant back to that time and ask the question: '*How was that parent feeling to act in such a way?*' usually the answer that arises is that the parent had some powerful negative emotion running, possibly from a pattern that started with their parents. Often it transpires that the parent who left believed that their child, even the whole family, would be better off without them. So their behaviour was not because they did not love or care. It was because they did not know how to deal with their feelings and negative beliefs about themselves. They did the only thing they felt they could do. In fact, in their own way, they did it out of love.

Move Past Your Psychology

Psychology has made some important contributions to the understanding of the workings of our minds, like the concept of projection and transference. It has effectively documented our defence mechanisms and given a wide range of labels to all kinds of behaviours. All this is to be celebrated. But there is still one aspect of our psychology we must keep in mind. We made it all up.

Our psychology is a hoax; to spend time in endless analysis is to study an illusion.

Sue says:

A few years ago an American friend of mine whose relationship had just ended came to stay. She told the story of how after years of expensive analysis her partner had discovered that he had a core pattern of abandonment. He had explored every possible facet of his core issue and then, even after all that, he went out and acted on it and 'abandoned' his partner by leaving her. Psychology can help us to uncover our patterns, it might even increase our awareness of why we do what we do but in the end we make the choices, and we have always done so. Often it is made to look like our psychology runs us. It is some beast that has us in its control and that will set up a strong victim stance. Yet at a deeper level it gives us an excuse to do what it is we want. It gives us control!

You can put yourself under a psychological microscope and dissect yourself to bits. But until you are willing to take responsibility for your feelings, feel them and reach the deeper understanding underneath them, you will be compelled to keep acting out your patterns. This, as we have said before, is a failure of intelligence.

Understanding psychology is undoubtedly very helpful. But in the final analysis we need to recognise we have the power of choice. How we choose, so it will be – and how it is now is what we have chosen it to be. We can always make a new and better choice.

Make Your Partner More Important Than Your Past

Let's look at an example of how these insidious patterns run a relationship. In this instance, we will take a behaviour like nagging. Usually the nagger, often (but not always) the woman, is chewing the arse off the nagged about something like getting them to stop playing golf, come home early or stop drinking.

What is going on here is that the nagged, by withdrawing from his partner, has made some past pain more important than his relationship, which has caused distance to grow. His actions are effectively saying to his wife: this past issue is more important than you, so I will spend my time where I don't have to feel bad. Typically, a women has a radar for such things. She feels the disconnect and therefore recognises her partner has made something else – work or golf or computers – more important than her. When this happens most women will start making their discontent known.

If the nagged one is smart, he will realise this. He could now make a choice, either continue to keep this ball of pain, this psychology between them, or he could make his partner the most important thing in his life and, energetically, move towards her.

This simple choice can end the whole issue and move the relationship forward. Just *the attitude and intention of making the relationship work*, of always stepping towards your partner, will melt away so much of our past programming. Once you have closed the distance with your partner and the bond is there, you will then find she will let you play all the golf you want, or he will let you shop to your heart's content. Either that, or you won't want to do so much golf or shopping; either way, the issue is over.

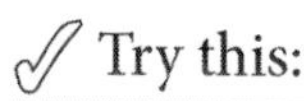

Choose to Extend Yourself to Others

One of the best choices we can make is to recognise that whatever is going on for us, there is someone around us in much more trouble. There is always someone better off, but also *worse* off, than you. What would we rather do, sit around and debate our psychology or go and help them? Every act like this, because it is an act of courage and service, will help us transcend another chunk of our psychology. We just need to remember to do it.

Give – But Not Out of Sacrifice

Making something more important than your partner, like football, shopping or whatever, is being indulgent. The opposite of indulgence is sacrifice. When we sacrifice, we are attempting to hide our taking under a mountain of apparent giving. This strategy leads to comments like: *'I did everything for him/her. I gave and gave and look how the son of a bitch treated me!'*

We may give in ninety-nine different ways. But that one desire to take something back undoes all that apparent giving. This is when we are 'giving to get'; our giving has an agenda to it and it will never work. It will never supply our happiness because we give up our lives to get others to meet our needs. So often we hear the refrain: *'But they should give back in some way, that is only fair. For all the things I have done for them, they should...'* Well, if you insist, try living that way and see if it leads to long-term success. In our experience, giving is unconditional. True love is when you just love someone. You pour love into them and it does not matter what they do or how they behave. Any form of condition changes our giving into taking. Now we are caught, until we make another decision.

A common story we hear with our clients is how someone in a relationship gave everything to their partner to support them through their training and then when they graduated they just took off with hardly a thank you.

This is a typical story of confusing taking, or sacrifice, with true giving. Underlying this story is a hidden agenda, which says: *'If I give then I will get something back.'* It is undeniable that what they were doing was an act of kindness and helpfulness but the hidden expectation of what will come back trashes the whole effort. The extent to which one partner goes into this level of sacrifice the other partner will balance them off by becoming increasingly indulgent. So the extent to which we go into sacrifice, into inequality and making it all about them, they will balance the relationship out by becoming indulgent, which is also making it all about them.

Through our giving we will get to know who we are. You will know when you are giving because that is what will come back to you. That is the natural cycle. But our giving has to come with no attachment to what we will get back. We are really being asked to become pure of heart! But then, what is the point of love if you don't share it?

Getting Out of Sacrifice

Sacrifice is when you feel you *have* to do something, so that you feel divided and in conflict about it. The task in hand then becomes difficult, time consuming and exhausting. Recognise that you have a choice here: You could choose to do it, or not to do it. Believing you don't have a choice will drive you back into sacrifice, which will continue to make you feel burdened and resentful. Once you choose, then it is no longer sacrifice. It is giving. You will know it is giving because what you give is what you get. Sometimes it is important to reverse this and realise that the opposite is also true: what you are getting is what you are giving!

Make Your Partner As Important As Your Children

If you ask people who they love the most, their partner or their children, the answer is, usually: 'My children, of course!' Parental love is obviously different to the love between a couple, but putting your child or children before your partner is not healthy for your relationship. One of the core principles we teach couples is: No matter what is happening, move *towards* your partner.

Remember the feelings of love you had with your partner when you first met them, all those honeymoon feelings of closeness, caring and sharing? We all know that we come out of this honeymoon stage and our issues come up between us. Now if you introduce a child into this mix usually one partner, or both, will develop that same relationship of great intimacy, caring and giving with the child – which is at odds with the relationship with their partner. This means there are some unresolved and unhealed issues going on in the parents' relationship. In a healthily bonded, loving family the feelings you have with your children are the same feelings you have with your partner. You might act differently – as would be appropriate – but the feelings of intimacy, caring and giving would be the same.

Imagine if your partner was caring, accepting, loving and concerned about you, and you behaved in this way towards them. That would be the essence of a true and meaningful relationship. So if these are not the predominant feelings, rather than substitute them with the love between you and your children, it is important that you take whatever steps need to be taken to return to that feeling of intimacy and love with your partner.

Having a child is a great exercise in making someone more important than yourself. When we create a loving and bonded family where everyone feels they are equally important, this bonding creates ease and success in the child's life, just as a loving and bonded relationship creates ease and success within our own lives.

Sue says:

Even before Jeff and I were actually splitting up, I was aware that my emotional happiness was more focused on our two children than on him. He was away so much, life seemed simpler

> and more loving when it was just the three of us. I could be more 'me' and I didn't resent doing anything for them the same way I did with Jeff. Of course this attitude increased the distance between Jeff and me. I realise now that, for the children, it was also a negative example of how a relationship works. It actually added to the split in the family because Jeff and I weren't resolving our issues. Instead we were deflecting them onto the children. I was using the children to fill that need for closeness and intimacy in me, which made things tough on them because the last thing children want to do is choose between their parents. In the years since Jeff and I got back together we have apologised to our children for this many times! We also know that our relationship now gives them a stronger foundation for their own partnerships.

Find Your Common Purpose

Why do we get into relationships, why do we share our lives with others? Deep down, we all know a relationship is our best chance for happiness. It is certainly our best chance for growth, for gaining wisdom and maturity.

It is wise to remind ourselves why we are in a relationship, or even this particular relationship. We need to ask ourselves: '*What is it I am trying to achieve by sharing my life with this person?*' We need to have this conversation with our partner because if we don't set a common purpose, our next fight could be our last one, our next fight could be a deal breaker.

✓ Try this:

Find the time to get together with your partner and ask each other: '*What is the purpose of us being together? What would we like to achieve?*'

Reach a joint understanding and agreement of where it is that you want to go in this partnership. Is it to find happiness, is it to find companionship and friendship, is it to achieve a true intimacy, is it to create a safe and loving space for family and friends? Agree this common purpose between yourselves, and have it fully understood and accepted. Once you have set this common purpose then everything that is in the way of achieving that goal will come to the surface. Now with awareness you can understand what you need to deal with in order to achieve this common purpose together.

It is helpful to review this common purpose and see how you are doing. As you near the achievement of your goals, you can set a new common purpose that is further down the road than the last one. Your relationship will then become a dynamic force moving forward with purpose. Without this your relationship can be like a crippled ship at sea, at the mercy of the forces of the wind and waves. It is only a matter of time before you strike a reef and flounder.

All we are really doing in this exercise is bringing to the surface and reminding ourselves of what we have already done on a subconscious level. We think we have not chosen what we want out of our relationship, but on a deeper level, we have. We might even be living with someone who has very different goals –

which could well explain some of our relationship difficulties.

See Each Other As Equals

When we meet someone for the first time, most of us automatically secretly assess whether they will be useful to us or not. We consider whether this person is someone we can take from, or whether they will take from us. Are we better than them, or are they better than us? Our ego selves don't really care which way it is, whether we are better or worse than someone else, just provided we are not equal.

When we were little, our ego developed from a sense of being separate from others. Our ego self cannot see us as equal, for without this sense of separation, it cannot even exist. Inequality always sets up sacrifice: If we see ourselves as better than our partner, then we need to take care of them, to carry them and so we go into sacrifice. Sooner or later we will react angrily to the build up of bad feelings and resentment this sacrifice brings.

The other way is to put ourselves below our partner, which again puts us into sacrifice, because now we put them on a pedestal and give up our lives to worship them. We will do that for a while until the pain of sacrifice gets too strong and we knock them off the pedestal, usually at the same time denying that it was us that put them there in the first place. We are so clever, we can even hide our belief in our superiority under our acts of inferiority.

Either way there is an inequality and many things can happen, but one thing that cannot happen is love. When there is equality, there is a natural connection, a level of bondedness which opens us up to giving and receiving love. Without equality this connection is lost and the flow of love is no longer possible.

We need to remember that we are equals. We are certainly different and have different gifts. In fact, we might even be a little further down the track, but we are no better or worse than others.

Choose Your Attitude

All our thoughts and actions are goal-orientated: they are either building up our lives or breaking them down. A simple change in attitude, as so many self-help and 'law of attraction' books tell us, can transform your world. Here are our top four that work for us. We suggest you remind yourself of them daily.

COMMIT:

To have a successful relationship we need to commit to our partner on a continuous basis – every day in fact – and to give up any ideas that we are superior or inferior to them. Whatever is going on, keep moving towards your partner, with gratitude, appreciation and tenderness, a few of the essential ingredients of love. Have the attitude and intention of making your relationship work.

BE WILLING:

We don't need to work it all out, understand all our neuroses, the intricate working of our minds, or have a PhD in psychology. No. All we need is willingness; the willingness to learn and to find a better way. When we are willing to open our minds and hearts and learn the lesson, then the teachers or books or the inspiration we need miraculously show up. The universe, as the saying goes, conspires to help you.

TRUST:

In our experience we are never put in any situation where there is no way out, *provided* we are willing to learn and change. As soon as we realise we are not right about a single thing we thought we were right about, then we can resign as our own teacher – and put our trust in the people and situations in our lives to show us exactly where all our misunderstandings are. Having the courage to stay with the 'what is' and work with it, builds up your trust in yourself and in life. We start to see that people aren't really out to get us, rather they are acting from their pain – and we learn to extend ourselves to them. As we give to life, it gives right back.

VALUE YOURSELF AND YOUR PARTNER:

During the years of work in this area, it has become apparent that the greatest block to our happiness and success is our self-esteem. Many of us hide a poor sense of our own value under hard work, or roles, or countless other compensations. We may be giving the outward appearance of having life handled but inside we know that is not the truth, and often so do our partners. But we can change this, and change it in a relatively simple way. The first step is to value the people and things in our lives. As we see value in all that surrounds us, we will start to know our own value. Being committed, willing and trusting enough to see the lesson in every situation, gives your whole life great value, leaving you filled with appreciation and gratitude.

Never, Ever Give Up

The current Dalai Lama once issued a statement called 'Never Give Up.' This is especially true in relationships because the purpose of our lives and our relationship is to find happiness, to find love and peace. Everything that is not happy, peaceful or loving will come to the surface sooner or later. This dynamic is inevitable. Whatever stands in the way has to be dealt with before we can achieve these goals.

So often when we are facing issues or aspects of our lives that are not working we adjust to the situation rather than tackle it. The reason things go wrong is to show us what we need to change, what we need to learn. If we refuse the lessons, or blame others, we are basically resigning. We are giving up.

When we start adjusting to situations we don't like, we are not dealing with what needs to be handled. Sooner or later we look back and wonder what happened to our lives. What happened to the love in our relationship? It dawns on us that we have spent a lifetime adjusting to what is going on, accommodating what should not be accommodated, until we have lost sight of everything we once thought was important. Each time we adjust we attack ourselves, our abilities and our own heartfelt desires. Tolerating what should not be tolerated is a sign of weakness. It is as bad as not tolerating what should be tolerated. So have courage and face what you need to face. Finding the courage to be true to ourselves and live the life we always wanted is within our power.

We need to follow our hearts and we need to fight for what we believe in. That doesn't mean we should fight the people around us. We learn not to fight our partner but to fight for our partnership; we do everything we can to improve our relationship, recognising it is the most important thing in our life. The rewards for having a great relationship will give you everything your heart desires. It will become the bedrock of your life where you will never feel alone again.

And Finally... When it is Time to Move On

Some relationships last a lifetime – and some relationships will not. Relationships are not about time, they are about growing (and no, we don't include one night stands in this dynamic!). The main purpose of all relationships is to learn about ourselves, develop and grow as people – to evolve. Once we have learned certain lessons for our personal evolution, sometimes it is time to move on.

You know it is a good break up when:

- You can be friends
- You both agree
- You don't resent the time you spent together
- You have grown and learned lessons
- You have a continuing good relationship
- Any children involved don't feel they have lost anything. In fact, if there are new partnerships the children actually feel they can have extra mums and dads
- There is no guilt or bad feelings

However, if there are any strong feelings of dislike in either partner, if you cannot bear to be in the same room together, or if there is an ocean of deadness and distance between you, then it means that the purpose of the relationship, however long it has lasted, has not been achieved. It means there are unlearned lessons and unresolved emotions that still need to be addressed. If not, they will only get played out in your next relationship. Or you might end up unable to attract a new relationship because you give up on them or feel too hurt to ever try again.

Of course, if you are in a physically, sexually, mentally or emotionally abusive relationship, then it is absolutely right to seek help and leave. Until one partner is brave enough to take such action then the abusive relationship will not change. It is important to live by the principle to not, to the best of your ability, hurt others and equally to not let others hurt you.

The key to a good break-up is always to take responsibility for yourself and your feelings – and, crucially, letting go of the need to be right.

In a good relationship break-up there is no blame. It cannot be that you are doing it 'right' and your soon-to-be-ex-partner is fighting you. If you have hired lawyers and are heading for a courtroom, you are in a fight – and in a fight, there are no winners. You need to recognise that you are both fighting; using different methods maybe, but you are both fighting. It has been our experience that if you give up the fight, if you give up being right, then your partner will give up the fight to the same degree. Putting your partner down or bad mouthing them in any way to friends and relations is part of the fight – even if you are bad mouthing them about the fact that they are fighting.

If there are children involved, it is important to recognise that, as their parents, you will be in relationship with each other for the rest of your lives. Then comes the question: are you going to do what it takes to make it a positive relationship, one that doesn't shatter your children or ask them to choose between you and take sides?

When it becomes clear that a relationship is ending, each partner subconsciously sets their intention about how the break up is going to be. If you don't make a *conscious* decision, you need to recognise that your subconscious decision is playing out in front of you right now; and that you could re-set your intention consciously at any time.

To have a good break up you both need to communicate honestly and continuously about your desires and wishes, your thoughts and emotions. You can also jointly set goals for what you really want and how you want it to be.

Be vigilant about the tendency to turn it into a fight. If you feel hurt or disappointed, you will be tempted to blame and shame the other person. Recognise the dynamic and get yourself back on track.

If there is a third party involved or a new relationship on the horizon then be up front about it. Don't be secretive but keep moving towards resolution and friendship. Avoid behaving in any way you might feel guilty about, because guilt is a destructive force in any relationship.

Make sure the break is clean and really finish the relationship. It might be easy to stay in business together, or you might be joint parents, but close the joint bank accounts, settle the finances and the paperwork. Share out whatever needs to be shared out so there is no lingering practical business between you – which is just a reflection of lingering emotional business.

Appreciate the lessons you have learned and acknowledge them to your partner. Coming to a clean and clear resolution is a much more effective way of building your life, so that you can use the past as a springboard into the future, rather than going back to ground level and starting all over again in the next relationship.

AFTERWORD

'I needed lessons in love. I still do, because nothing could be simpler, nothing could be harder, than love.'

Jeanette Winterson

Every Problem is a Relationship Problem

We all need lessons in love. Good relationships don't just happen, they take application and learning. In truth, each relationship is either getting better or getting worse. It is moving in one direction or the other, even when on the surface it appears to be staying in one place. The direction is an outcome of our choices. If we get it right, our relationship will become the source of our greatest happiness: a source of fun, love, deep friendship and profound intimacy. It becomes the bedrock of our lives and allow us to excel in our endeavours and give us support and meaning in times of our greatest hardships. Every problem we have in our life is a relationship problem. If we can find the echo of a problem occurring in our wider world and transform it within our relationship, it will easily resolve in our wider world. That is the power of a growing and evolving relationship.

We hope and pray that some of the lessons in this book will give you back the spark; give you back the meaning and the love of life that is part of your nature. When people get old they do not run out of energy because of their years, they run out of energy because of the mental burdens they carry, the regrets, the guilt, the unsaid thoughts, the unfulfilled life. It is never too late to turn that around, so that when you look at the challenges in your life and you see what mountains need to be climbed, you recognise that you have come to be that person. You have come to be that brave, that talented, that strong. When you look at your life and recognise that only a fearless paladin could overcome the challenges, then you accept that is who you have come to be.

Sue says:

When I look back, I wonder how it has happened that my original expectations of how love works have been so comprehensively surpassed. Thank you, Jeff, for being the gateway to a new sense of personal happiness and peace. I know I am stronger in myself now because we have pushed the boundaries and learned more and more about the good, the bad, and the ugly parts of ourselves. You have always been the brave one, the catalyst for growth and learning, and I feel blessed that we are hand in hand on the journey.

Jeff says:

This book has been a process for us and now sitting in a lunch break during a seminar in Taiwan at the end of 2011 co-facilitating with you I have time to reflect back on our path. It has not always been easy and there have been great highs and lows. I fully recognise I would not have made it but for your love and support, Sue. Even as I write this we are going through some challenges in our lives but I know we will make it through. A loving relationship does make a man fearless and gives him direction and for these two gifts I thank you, my eternal partner, from the bottom of my heart. I am so grateful that you have been willing to allow me to take my place beside you as we share this path.